The Foreign

STUDIES IN ECONOMIC, SOCIAL AND POLITICAL CHANGE:
THE REPUBLIC OF CHINA

Understanding Communist China:
Communist China Studies in the United States
and the Republic of China, 1949–1978
  Tai-chun Kuo and Ramon H. Myers

Phoenix and the Lame Lion:
Modernization in Taiwan and Mainland China, 1950–1980
  Alan P. L. Liu

The Great Transition:
Political and Social Change in the Republic of China
  Hung-mao Tien

A Unique Relationship:
The United States and the Republic of China
Under the Taiwan Relations Act
  Ramon H. Myers, editor

The Foreign Factor:
The Multinational Corporation's Contribution to the
Economic Modernization of the Republic of China
  Chi Schive

About the Author

Chi Schive is a Professor of Economics in the Department and Graduate Institute of Economics, College of Law, at National Taiwan University, Taiwan, Republic of China. He was formerly Professor and Dean in the College of Management, National Central University, Taipei, Taiwan; a Fellow of the Mont Pelerin Society, 1982; and a Visiting Scholar at the Hoover Institution, 1986.

The Foreign Factor

The Multinational Corporation's Contribution
to the Economic Modernization of the
Republic of China

Chi Schive

Hoover Institution Press

Stanford University   Stanford, California

Hoover Press Publication 389

First printing, 1990

96 95 94 93 92 91 90   9 8 7 6 5 4 3 2 1

Simultaneous first paperback printing, 1990

96 95 94 93 92 91 90   9 8 7 6 5 4 3 2 1

Manufactured in the United States of America

Printed on acid-free paper

Library of Congress Cataloging in Publication Data
Hsüeh, Ch'i.
    The foreign factor: the multinational corporation's contribution
to the economic modernization of the Republic of China / Chi Schive.
        p.   cm. — (Hoover Press publication ; 389)
    Includes bibliographical references.
    ISBN 0-8179-8891-2 — ISBN 0-8179-8892-0 (pbk.)
    1. International business enterprises—Taiwan.   2. Investments, Foreign—Taiwan.   3. Technology transfer—Economic aspects—Taiwan.   4. Taiwan—Economic   conditions—1945-   5. Taiwan—Economic policy—1945-   I. Title.
HD2912.H78 1990   89-71673
338.8'8851249—dc20   CIP

Contents

Tables and Figures

Preface

The development of this book can be likened to the growth of a river: it is the confluence of many sources.

In the fall of 1974, I went to Albany, New York, with Asim Erdilek, then my graduate adviser at Case Western Reserve University. There we jointly delivered a paper titled "An Empirical Study of Cross-Direct Foreign Investment" at the inaugural meeting of the Eastern Economic Association. During that meeting, the idea of writing my dissertation on multinational corporations in Taiwan emerged. Two years later, I returned to Taiwan to conduct a survey on foreign firms in Taiwan, which became a part of my dissertation, "Direct Foreign Investment, Technology Transfer and Linkage Effects: A Case Study of Taiwan." That study was the antecedent of the present book.

After completing my graduate work, I continued to explore the effects of direct foreign investment (DFI) in Taiwan, broadening several aspects of the original study. First, four case studies on technical cooperation at the industrial level were carried out between 1980 and 1983. In 1981, I examined local content (the local purchasing behavior of foreign firms), an issue related to linkage theory. In 1982, I took a fresh look at the factor proportion problems caused by DFI. Taiwan's outward investment (specifically, the emerging native multinationals) received special attention in studies I undertook in 1981 and 1985. By that time, a fairly comprehensive picture of DFI in Taiwan was beginning to take shape.

In 1984 I met Dr. Ramon H. Myers, of the Hoover Institution on War, Revolution and Peace, who was spending his sabbatical year at Sun Yat-sen University in Taiwan. In the course of our discussions, he suggested that I present my findings on DFI in Taiwan to a wider audience by compiling my studies into a book. A year later, when I was a visiting scholar at Harvard's Yenching Institute, Dr. Myers developed a program that enabled me to spend some time at the Hoover Institution to work on that book. The bulk of the work was done in the summer of 1986, though the final version was not completed until the fall of 1988.

In addition to Dr. Myers, I must thank many other people for helping and encouraging me in my study of DFI over the years. Dr. Erdilek first brought the topic to my attention when I was looking about for a dissertation topic. Professor Kuo-shu Liang, then vice chairman of the Research, Development and Evaluation Commission of the Executive Yuan of the Republic of China, provided the grant that underwrote the field survey. Three successive chairmen of National Taiwan University's Department of Economics, Professors Yen Hwa, Cheng-cherng Chen and Ta-ho Lin, all gave me every assistance necessary to the completion of this book and, even more important, encouraged me in my study. The Investment Commission of the Ministry of Economic Affairs supported many of these studies financially and provided necessary data. Needless to say, I owe much to those professors at National Taiwan University and Case Western Reserve University who fostered my interest in, and my knowledge of economics. They have my heartfelt thanks. Last but not least, Professors Gustav Ranis, W. L. Ting, K.W. Hsueh, and R.S. Yet, with whom I have jointly written papers collected in this volume, deserve more than an acknowledgement.

Because this book includes previously published papers, I am indebted to the several publishers for their permission to include those articles here. I wish to thank the University of Wisconsin Press; Lexington Books, a division of D. C. Heath & Co.; the College of Business Administration of the University of Hawaii; the Department of Economics of National Taiwan University, publisher of *Economic Essays* (later renamed *Taiwan Economic Review*); and the National Science Council of the Republic of China.

Finally, the time spent in writing the papers and preparing the book has taken a heavy toll on my family life. By way of minor compensation, this book is dedicated to my wife Jane and to our two sons, Ping and Yu.

1

Introduction

Taiwan, a province of the Republic of China (ROC), has attracted widespread attention by its successful economic development over the past three decades. Between 1953 and 1987, the island's economy achieved an annual growth rate of 8.8 percent, propelling it into the ranks of the newly industrializing countries. In an age in which many nations struggle with little success to develop economically, what has been special about Taiwan's experience? How was it able to expand so rapidly? What policies did Taiwan implement to sustain such growth?

The reasons for Taiwan's success do not lie in its physical attributes. The island totals some 36,000 square kilometers—somewhere between the area of Belgium and that of the Netherlands, or roughly the size of Connecticut. With 535 persons per square kilometer in 1985, Taiwan's population density is very high: with the exception of the city-states—for example, Hong Kong and Singapore—the island's population density is second only to that of Bangladesh (692/sq. km. in 1985) and considerably above the densities of the Netherlands (355/sq. km. in 1985) and South Korea (434/sq. km. in 1985). Because two-thirds of the island consists of nonarable mountains, Taiwan's geographical characteristics do not favor agriculture.

Nonetheless, economic growth has raised the per capita GNP from $486 in 1953 to $3761 in 1987 (at 1981 prices and exchange rates), or at current exchange rates, to $4989 in 1987, due to the significant rise of the New Taiwan (NT) dollar against the U.S. dollar. It is predicted that Taiwan's per capita income will parallel Italy's by the end of this century,[1] qualifying Taiwan as a developed country (DC) and making it second in Asia only to Japan (see table 1).

1.1 One Contributing Factor: Direct Foreign Investment

The rapid growth of Taiwan's economy demands explanation. Many studies have been done, ranging from those focusing on the role of the agricultural sector in the earlier stages of Taiwan's development (Lee 1971) to much more comprehensive studies covering trade, industry, and labor through the mid-1970s (Galenson 1979) and after (Kuo 1983; Galenson 1985; Lau 1986). With the exception of a still limited discussion in one chapter in Galenson's book (Ranis and Schive 1985), none of these studies has adequately analyzed the far-reaching effect of direct foreign investment (DFI) on Taiwan's economy.

A thorough investigation of the role of DFI in Taiwan's development is clearly warranted. DFI can provide sources of additional capital that can alleviate the capital shortages of less-developed countries.[2] At first glance, figures for DFI in Taiwan may not appear significant.

TABLE 1   MAIN ECONOMIC INDICATORS OF TAIWAN, 1965–1987

	1965	1987	Growth rate, 1965–1987 (percent)
Population (million)	12.6	19.7	2.09
GNP ($ billion, at 1981 prices)	10.5	97.5	9.23
Industrial output	—	—	14.08
Manufacturing employment (1,000)	612	2,809	7.40
Manufacturing/GDP (at current prices)	20.1	43.48	—
Manufacturing/total employment	16.4	35.02	—
Export/GNP (at current prices)	18.70	54.89	—
Import/GNP (at current prices)	21.71	35.38	—
Trade/GNP (at current prices)	40.41	90.27	—

SOURCES: Council for Economic Planning and Development, R.O.C., *Taiwan Statistical Data Book, 1985*; Department of Statistics, Ministry of Economic Affairs (hereafter MOEA), *Domestic and Foreign Express Report of Economic Statistics and Indicators, 1988*.

TABLE 2 DFI CONTRIBUTION TO TAIWAN'S CAPITAL FORMATION, 1965–1983
(UNITS: $ MILLION AND PERCENT)

	ARRIVED DFI		DFI AS PERCENT OF DOMESTIC CAPITAL FORMATION		
Period	*Manufacturing*	*Total*	*Total*	*Manufacturing*	*Private, total*
1965–1968	60.6	75.8	2.20	4.70	3.31
1969–1972	161.9	202.4	4.32	7.33	5.47
1973–1976	266.8	333.5	1.74	4.25	3.27
1977–1980	414.3	517.9	1.37	4.27	2.50
1981–1983	384.8	481.0	1.35	3.86	2.79
1984–1986	740.4	925.5	2.51	5.77	4.46

SOURCE: Table A-1.
NOTE: DFI in manufacturing is estimated as 80 percent of total arrived DFI.

When DFI started picking up in the mid-1960s (see Chapter Two), its proportional contribution to the country's total capital formation ranged from insignificant to moderate—from 1.37 to 4.32 percent during the period of 1965–1986, with a declining trend that extended from the 1970s until recently. Because DFI came from private investors and was concentrated in the manufacturing sector, the share of DFI in private capital formation was higher—between 2.50 and 5.47 percent during the same period—but this share also declined during the 1970s. The contribution of DFI to the manufacturing total was even higher, ranging from 7.33 percent at its peak in 1969–1972 to 3.86 percent in the 1981–1983 subperiod. As these figures show, DFI has not made a significant contribution to Taiwan's total capital formation, except moderately in the manufacturing sector. Moreover, the relative importance of DFI's contribution to capital formation in Taiwan has declined between the 1970s and the last period, 1984–1986 (see table 2).

The contribution made to GNP by foreign firms (defined as local companies with any amount of foreign capital) is greater than the above figures would imply, however. For example, a total of 795 foreign firms contributed 8.34 percent of Taiwan's total GNP in 1979. While many foreign firms are joint ventures—and the definition of DFI we have used here lends itself to overestimation of DFI's role in the economy—the weighted figure for foreign ownership still amounts to about half the unweighted figure.[3]

Other indicators, either weighted or unweighted, are more significant. For example, exports of foreign firms accounted for around 20 percent (with a definite declining trend) of the country's total exports between 1974 and 1982; weighted figures for the same period range from 9.1 to 15.5 percent during that period. Foreign firms' contribution (unweighted) to manufacturing employment ran from around 16 percent at the peak between 1977 and 1979 to 8.79 percent at the low point in 1985 (see table 3). These data reveal unmistakably that DFI has played an active and important role in Taiwan's development, particularly in the areas of employment and exports. How these results were achieved is an intriguing question.

1.2   DFI and Technology Transfer

Apart from the practical reasons for examining the role played by an important factor in Taiwan's rapidly growing economy, the study of DFI in conjunction with technology transfer serves other purposes. Technological change or progress has long been recognized as the most important factor affecting a country's growth. Many empirical studies have shown that the accumulation of primary resources, mainly capital and labor, does not contribute to economic growth to the same degree as improved efficiency, whether embodied in one factor or in the system as a whole (Solow 1957; Denison 1967).

Technological change has contributed greatly to Taiwan's growth. According to an empirical study using the same approach for 23 less-developed countries (LDCs), Taiwan, with 38 percent, had the largest proportion of GDP growth that could not be accounted for by an increase in labor and capital (Maddison 1970). Some more recent studies show an even higher proportion (Kuo 1983, chap. 11). Two similar studies called for a case study of Taiwan to fill the gaps in our knowledge about technological change (Nelson 1974; Spencer and Wonoiak 1970).

There are several ways to upgrade the technological level of an economy. Emphasis may be placed on the indigenous scientific community, or more precisely, on the different roles played by government, business, universities, and individuals (Nelson 1974; Spencer 1970). In an open developing economy, however, new technology may be more easily acquired from abroad by imitation, licensing, DFI, or free goods, than internally by self-development (Johnson 1968).

TABLE 3   DFI CONTRIBUTION TO TAIWAN'S GNP, EXPORTS, AND EMPLOYMENT, 1974–1982 (UNITS: $ MILLION, PERCENT)

GNP DUE TO FOREIGN FIRMS

		UNWEIGHTED			WEIGHTED BY FOREIGN OWNERSHIP		
Year	Number of foreign firms	Total	Percent of national total	Percent of mfg.	Total	Percent of national total	Percent of mfg.
1974	723	882	6.20	21.37	—	—	—
1977	747	1,492	7.66	24.31	—	—	—
1979	795	2,696	8.34	28.00	1,328	4.27	14.3
1982	847	2,570	5.62	19.09	1,253	2.74	9.3
1985	618	3,546	6.00	13.02	1,476	2.50	5.5

EXPORTS DUE TO FOREIGN FIRMS

	UNWEIGHTED		WEIGHTED	
Year	Total	Percent of national	Total	Percent of national
1974	1,196	21.8	854	15.5
1977	1,960	20.9	1,269	12.1
1979	3,284	20.4	2,030	10.8
1982	4,275	19.7	2,572	9.1
1985	4,862	15.8	3,386	11.0

EMPLOYMENT DUE TO FOREIGN FIRMS (1,000 PERSONS)

	UNWEIGHTED			WEIGHTED		
Year	Total	Percent of national	Percent of manufacturing	Total	Percent of national	Percent of manufacturing
1974	245	4.46	15.78	—	—	—
1977	298	4.98	16.28	189	3.16	10.33
1979	357	5.55	16.65	210	3.26	9.79
1982	326	4.78	14.63	189	2.77	8.48
1985	234	3.09	8.79	148	1.96	5.55

SOURCE: *An Analysis of the Operation and Impacts of Foreign Enterprises*, various issues. (Investment Commission, Ministry of Economic Affairs)

NOTE: Exports due to foreign firms exclude indirect exports.

Among these four channels of international technology transfer, "the most successful examples of the rapid transfer of technology are found in the activities of the subsidiaries which are established by Western firms in underdeveloped countries" (Svennilson 1967, p. 179). In fact, "the essence of direct foreign investment is the transmission to the 'host' country of a package of capital, managerial skills, and technical knowledge" (Johnson 1972, p. 2). If that is the case, we should be able to find abundant evidence for links between DFI and technology transfer. Given the multidimensional character of DFI, what are the ramifications of technology transferred through DFI? A country case study will surely enhance our understanding of the complicated and very important phenomenon of technology transfer.

1.3   The Need for a Case Study on Taiwan

The essential position occupied by foreign firms in Taiwan's economic development, particularly as regards likely technology transfer, calls for a comprehensive case study on Taiwan. Several other factors are equally important. First, Taiwan's economy has undergone several internal changes over the past two decades or so. For instance, since the disappearance of surplus labor by the end of the 1960s, the Taiwanese economy has not only become increasingly dependent upon trade, but has also begun to build trade surpluses; and heavy industry has replaced light industry (Scitovsky 1986; Schive, in press). What role has DFI played in these changes in Taiwan's economy?

Second, DFI is not a one-way flow. Over the years, native multinational corporations (MNCs) have proliferated. What are the industry-wide and individual characteristics of those native multinationals? What are the causes of these corporations' going multinational, and what are its effects? What are the prospects for this new trend? These questions about Taiwan's outward investment must be answered in order to fully explore DFI's impact on Taiwan's economy.

The third factor calling for a case study on Taiwan is the ready availability of data and the consequent reliability of conclusions drawn from them. The Investment Commission of the Ministry of Economic Affairs has, since 1974, conducted an annual survey of foreign firms in Taiwan. The survey data cover each company's main operational and financial statistics, providing the most reliable and comprehensive information available on DFI activity. The wealth of these data makes possible the study of many difficult questions, such as the dynamic aspect of linkage issues, the changing role of DFI in terms of transferring and diffusing foreign technology, the features of foreign-derived technology, and so on. Findings from so solid a set of data would be of sufficient value to merit an empirical study.

1.4   Contents of the Study

A review of DFI inflows into Taiwan over the past years is a necessary preliminary to the study of DFI and technology transfer in Taiwan's development. The trend and sources of DFI inflow, industrial structure, capital formation, and ownership structure will be examined, after this introductory chapter, in Chapter Two.

Our examination of technology transfer due to DFI begins by investigating the extent to which foreign and national firms have received foreign technology. (National firms are those without any foreign-capital participation in their capital structure.) Then foreign technology is analyzed in relation to new products. Because technology includes managerial skills, of which marketing is an important one, the export market channels of foreign and national firms will be compared. Technical cooperation is another important channel for acquiring foreign technology in which DFI may be involved. Foreign investors may abuse their positions as parent companies to overprice the technology sold to their subsidiaries. That situation will be investigated with regard to Taiwan.

In the framework of neoclassical economic analysis, the main concern is the efficiency of resource allocation. Did DFI tend to improve that efficiency, or to cause it to deteriorate? That comparison will be made between national and foreign firms at the aggregate, industrial, and product levels. The study emphasizes the difference between foreign firms' exporting activities and their production for domestic markets. The implications for employment are drawn in Chapter Four.

Chapter Five is a case study of the Taiwan Singer Company. In this chapter, the process of technology diffusion and its effects are examined in detail. It is important to learn what the conditions and limitations of technology transfer through foreign investment are. This is accomplished by studying the success of Taiwan Singer.

DFI has been condemned for its enclavism, that is, the lack of contact between the foreign and domestic sectors (between the sector of the economy occupied by foreign firms and the rest of the economy). Has that been true for Taiwan? The effects of linkage are examined, and the enclavistic aspects of DFI are analyzed in both static and dynamic frameworks by focusing on changes in foreign firms' local content. A study of the determinants of foreign firms' local purchasing behavior is included.

During the 1970s, when, according to many indicators, the relative position of foreign firms in Taiwan's economy stabilized or even declined, the emerging large native firms became multinationals. What have been their rationales in expanding abroad? How do they survive? What are the prospects for this new trend? These questions provide the focus for Chapter Seven.

The last chapter presents the study's conclusions, interprets its results, compares the findings of this and other studies, and addresses several policy issues.

2

The Inflow of Direct
Foreign Investment into Taiwan

The flow of both private and nonprivate foreign capital into Taiwan began in its colonial period (Ranis and Schive 1985, pp. 87–89). In 1939, for instance, Japanese owned 18.4 percent of all companies with more than five employees, and in 1941 they controlled 91 percent of all paid-up capital in private business. The colonial government also raised funds from Japan and in the New York stock market to finance its public investment projects (Chang 1980).

This chapter, however, focuses on Taiwan's economic development since 1952,[1] examining the trend and composition of modern DFI inflow. By *composition of foreign investment* we mean the sources, industrial distribution, capital formation, and ownership structure of that investment.

2.1 The Trend of DFI Inflow into Taiwan

In 1952, the government promulgated two sets of regulations to guide overseas Chinese investment: Regulations for the Encouragement of Investment in Productive Enterprises by Overseas Chinese and Chinese Residents in Hong Kong and Macao; and Regulations Governing the Importation of Commodities with Self-Provided Exchange by Overseas Chinese for the Purpose of Making Investment in Productive Enterprise. It may be noted that these two regulations were born more out of necessity than out of a well-articulated attempt to attract investment; five of the regulated investments had been approved even before the law took effect.

The first overseas Chinese investment was by a Hong Kong–based paint manufacturer who began operating in 1951, bringing in a total of HK$46,900. Westinghouse, the first non-Chinese investor, put US$1.88 million into equipment for Taiwan Power Co. in 1953. This investment, too, was made before the imposition of legal guidelines.

The Statute for Investment by Non-Chinese Foreigners was promulgated in 1954. A year later, a similar law, the Statute for Investment by Overseas Chinese, became effective. Both statutes were generous toward foreign investment. There were no restrictions on foreign ownership; a broadly defined range of industry was open to foreign investors; and used machinery and materials could be converted into capital. The only major difference between the two statutes is that overseas Chinese were allowed to invest in any industry—real estate and the service industries in particular—provided they did not waive the privilege of foreign-exchange settlement. Overall, a hospitable environment for DFI has existed since the early 1950s.

Figure 1 shows the trend of DFI arrivals between 1960 and 1986, as reflected in the balance of payments. Before 1960, DFI arrivals fluctuated between $0.5 million at the low point in 1955, and $1.1 million at the peak in 1959 (see table A-1). Data for arrivals, not approvals, are used in this analysis because the arrived capital amounted to around 45 percent of that approved during the observed period. There were two main reasons for this. First, the data for approvals refer to total capital committed, but paid-up capital is allowed to arrive any time within three years after approval; therefore, there is always a lag between the two figures. Second, many approved investment plans never materialized, including some multimillion dollar projects like the proposed Swedish investment in the China Shipbuilding Company, the Austrian investment in China Steel, and the deferred and reduced investment by Toyota.[2] The significant difference between these two sets of data argues against the use of approval data to assess DFI in Taiwan unless structural analyses are conducted to compensate for insufficiently detailed data on arrived investment.

The trend of DFI reveals several interesting points. First, there seems to have been a clearly increasing trend for arrived DFI since 1966. What made that year significant was the establishment of the first export processing zone (EPZ) in the vicinity of Kaohsiung, Taiwan's largest harbor. Two more were added five years later. Between

FIGURE 1   ARRIVED DIRECT FOREIGN INVESTMENT, 1960–1986

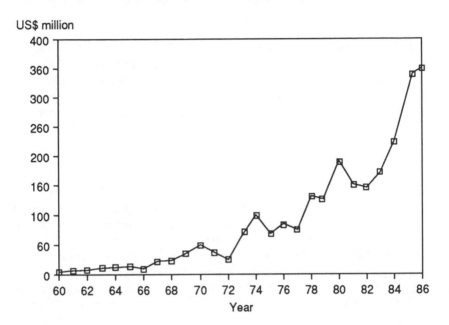

1966 and 1970, the first EPZ alone attracted a total of $32.7 million in DFI, constituting 80 percent of total capital arrivals in EPZs, and 23 percent of total arrived DFI. Another policy that has had the same effect in attracting export-oriented DFI calls for setting up bonded factories. In both cases, import duties are waived, provided all products are exported. Both policies have given a significant push to the inflow of DFI, particularly that intended for use in the production of exports.

Second, the post-1966 increasing trend of DFI seems to have faltered in 1972, 1975, and 1982. The first drop could have been due to international political changes unfavorable to Taiwan: in 1972, a year after the Republic of China lost its seat in the United Nations to mainland China. As for 1975 and 1982, both were recession years in Taiwan, in which economic growth rates dropped as low as 4.3 and 3.3 percent, respectively. Both political stability and domestic economic conditions, therefore, have had a great bearing on arrivals of DFI.

The political factor, which can affect Taiwan's ability to attract DFI in both ways, has received wide attention. Back in the 1950s, Jacoby

noted that "only after 1958, . . . when the Republic of China had demonstrated its defensive strength against Communist China in the Formosa Strait, did foreign private capital expand" (Jacoby 1968, p. 100).
In the 1960s, Schreiber compared Taiwan's political stability with that
of six other countries, and concluded that Taiwan was ahead of Mexico, Brazil, Nigeria, and Libya in that regard, but, as expected, behind
the United Kingdom and Japan (Schreiber 1970, p. 85). In his study of
Asian LDCs, Koh asked American export-oriented companies with
subsidiaries in Singapore, Taiwan, or Hong Kong to indicate the most
important factors influencing their decisions to locate there. For Taiwan, political stability was the third most important reason, after low
labor costs and tax incentives (Koh 1973). In brief, Taiwan's internal
political stability may have helped lure foreign investors in the 1960s
and thereafter.

In December 1978, another significant political event, the breaking
off of formal diplomatic relations between the Republic of China and
the United States, took place. The dramatic change in the position of
the Republic of China in the international political arena could,
obviously, have had far-reaching effects on the inflow of DFI into
Taiwan. The uncertainty caused by the United States' withdrawal of
its recognition of the Republic of China has, however, been reduced by
follow-up arrangements between the two countries, including the
U.S. Congress's passage of the Taiwan Act, which provides a limited
guarantee of Taiwan's security, and by the setting up of quasi-official
agencies in both countries to facilitate a wide range of relationships
between them. An economic factor proved equally important in pre-
venting a decline of DFI in Taiwan during that period. Economic conditions in Taiwan during 1978 and 1979 were extremely good, with the
country experiencing its highest growth rate ever, 13.9 percent, in
1978. Because DFI—both investment targeting the domestic market,
and that represented by the retained earnings of existing firms, which
constituted an increasing share of total arrived DFI (see section 2.4)—
responded positively to Taiwan's domestic economic conditions, the
immediate effect on DFI of the unfavorable political changes of 1979
was held to a minimum, as figure 1 attests.

2.2 Sources of DFI in Taiwan

A quarter of the total DFI in Taiwan during the period 1952–1987 came
from overseas Chinese. During the 1980s, however, that share
dropped significantly, falling to only 10 percent. In the non-Chinese

investment, U.S. capital was in the lead, making up 31 percent of the total, followed by Japan's 24 percent, Europe's 13 percent, and 12 percent from other sources. As regards trends in the sources of DFI, U.S. capital's share declined through the latest subperiod, 1981–1987, while the shares of Japan and Others increased. European investment rose through the 1960s and 1970s and continued to expand faster than the average in the 1980s.

In interpreting sources of DFI, it may be noted that several U.S. investments were made through U.S. subsidiaries in other countries: Ford's Taiwan venture was in association with Canada Ford; Gulf's investment was linked with Bermuda Gulf; and part of Singer's investment was financed by Swedish Singer. A rough estimate of the data bias against U.S. investment would be around 4 percent, which is not enough to alter the above observations.

2.3 Size and Ownership of DFI in Taiwan

By 1987, a total of 1,944 applications by overseas Chinese investors and 2,303 applications by non-Chinese foreigners had been approved. Among non-Chinese foreigners, U.S. investors accounted for 15 percent of the investment projects, or 635 projects; Japan, with the largest share, accounted for 28 percent, or 1,195 cases; and Europe and Others shared the rest, with 4 and 7 percent, respectively (see table 4).

The sizes of investments varied with their sources. As of 1987, the average non-Chinese investment was $2.56 million, much larger than the average $0.74 million of overseas Chinese. Among non-Chinese investors, European investments were the largest, averaging $5.43 million; followed by U.S. investments ($3.57 million) and Others ($3.07 million). The smallest non-Chinese investments, averaging $1.49 million, came from Japan.

The variations in size of investment reflect the relationships between the investors and the host country. It is to be expected that investments by overseas Chinese would be the smallest, because, to a large extent, those investors are not "foreigners," and are not treated as such. Their great familiarity with Taiwan's economy and their close connection with the local people facilitate their participation, so that even a relatively small investment can achieve their goals. Another relevant factor in this regard is that most of the overseas Chinese investors are from Hong Kong or Southeast Asian countries.

Japanese investors share many of these same characteristics with overseas Chinese. During the 50-year period of Japan's colonial rule,

TABLE 4   APPROVED DFI BY SOURCE, 1952–1987
(UNITS: $ MILLION, CASES)

Source	1952–1960		1961–1970		1971–1980		1981–1987		1952–1987	
	Amount	Cases	Amount	Cases	Amount	Cases	Amount	Cases	Amount	Cases
Overseas Chinese	10 (30)	54 (70)	153 (29)	647 (53)	801 (37)	774 (53)	471 (10)	469 (31)	1435 (20)	1944 (46)
Foreigners:	23 (70)	23 (30)	373 (71)	564 (47)	1358 (63)	675 (47)	4160 (90)	1041 (69)	5914 (80)	2303 (54)
U.S.	21 (62)	12 (15)	221 (42)	144 (12)	534 (25)	173 (12)	1492 (32)	306 (20)	2268 (31)	635 (15)
Japan	2 (8)	10 (13)	87 (16)	376 (31)	369 (17)	370 (26)	1325 (29)	439 (29)	1783 (24)	1195 (28)
Europe	— (—)	0 (0)	36 (7)	16 (1)	225 (10)	46 (3)	683 (15)	112 (8)	944 (13)	174 (4)
Others	0 (0)	1 (1)	29 (6)	28 (2)	230 (11)	86 (6)	660 (14)	184 (12)	919 (12)	299 (7)
Total	**33**	**78**	**526**	**1,211**	**2,159**	**1,449**	**4,631**	**558**	**7,349**	**4,247**
	(100)	**(100)**	**(100)**	**(100)**	**(100)**	**(100)**	**(100)**	**(100)**	**(100)**	**(100)**

SOURCE: Investment Commission, MOEA, *Statistics on Overseas Chinese and Foreign Investment, Technical Corporation, Outward Investment, Outward Technical Cooperation.*

the Japanese not only learned a great deal about Taiwan's economy, language, and culture, but also built up a cordial relationship with the natives. This unique relationship, based largely on personal contact, helps reduce both risk and investment size.

Europeans, on the other hand, have no such connections, and as a result their investments tend to be much larger. The average sizes of investment from U.S. sources and Others lie somewhere between those for Japanese and Europeans.

As for the ownership structure of DFI, U.S. sources and Europeans in particular clearly preferred majority control, or even wholly-owned ventures. Investors from other regions also showed the same tendency toward majority ownership, according to the 1985 data, but their rate of participation in companies of which they owned no more than 60 percent tended to be higher than that by U.S. and European ventures.

Japanese investors, on the other hand, preferred joint ventures, especially those with near-equal ownership (with foreign ownership at between 40 and 59 percent). Although overseas Chinese showed no strong preference for equal ownership, their ownership behavior was otherwise similar to that of Japanese investors.

The explanations given above for variation in size of investment by investor region can also be applied here. In fact, a positive correlation between these two findings exists: that is, a majority-owned foreign firm tends to commit more capital than a minority-owned firm does, given identical company size and financial structures. This helps explain why non-Japanese, non-Chinese foreigners tend to make larger investments than overseas Chinese and Japanese (see table 5).

2.4 Capital Composition of DFI in Taiwan

According to article 3 of the Statute, foreign capital may include: (1) foreign currency; (2) permissible imports of domestically needed machinery, equipment, and materials; (3) receipts of technical know-how or acquisition of patents; and (4) reinvested earnings. In 1965, imports of machinery and materials accounted for a large share of foreign capital, but that share has declined significantly since 1969. Investments in the form of machinery and materials were at first replaced by an increase in currency as the form of the invested capital; that increased use of currency has, in turn, been supplanted by reinvested earnings. These changes have a wide range of implications (see table 6).

TABLE 5   OWNERSHIP STRUCTURE OF FOREIGN ENTERPRISES, 1985
           (UNIT: PERCENT)

Investment Source	<40%	40–59%	60–99%	100%
Overseas Chinese	23.3	13.7	34.7	28.3
Foreigners:	18.9	28.5	19.1	33.5
U.S.	13.4	21.5	14.1	51.0
Japanese	21.1	34.2	21.4	23.2
European	15.8	15.8	23.7	44.7
Others	20.8	22.1	15.6	41.5

SOURCE: Investment Commission, MOEA, *An Analysis of the Operations and Economic Impacts of Foreign Enterprises,* 1985.

TABLE 6   CAPITAL COMPOSITION OF DFI, 1965–1983
           (UNIT: PERCENT)

Year	Currency	IMPORTS			Technical know-how	Reinvested earnings
		Machinery	Material	Total		
1965	28.6	50.0	21.4	71.4	0.0	—
1969	84.9	8.8	2.1	10.8	—	4.2
1972	87.9	4.3	0.5	4.8	—	7.3
1975	63.2	2.0	0.2	2.2	—	34.6
1979	81.6	1.1	0.2	1.3	—	17.1
1981	—	—	—	—	—	35.2
1983	—	—	—	—	—	26.5
1984	—	—	—	—	—	38.1
1985	—	—	—	—	—	19.5
1986	—	—	—	—	—	15.5

SOURCES: Data for 1965 from Liu 1971, p. 51; other data from the Central Bank of China.
NOTE: No breakdown of DFI capital is available for 1978–1983.

First, 50 percent of the DFI capital brought into Taiwan in 1965 in the form of machinery may have been used equipment. Strassman's study of DFI in Latin America in the 1960s found that "among American subsidiaries, 79 percent of those in Mexico and 57 percent of those in Puerto Rico used second-hand machines" (Strassman 1968, p. 211). He showed, furthermore, that about three-fifths of foreign firms used second-hand machinery, while only about one-third of national firms did so. Taiwan's situation may well be the same as that of the Latin American countries in the 1960s.

There are several advantages to using old machinery. The most obvious consideration is the difference in cost between old and new equipment. While this advantage might be beneficial to indigenous investors, foreign investors exploited it by selling that equipment to their subsidiaries at higher prices than they could charge elsewhere,[3] given the inequality of the seller's and the buyer's bargaining positions and the imperfect market for used machinery (James 1974). On the other hand, while smaller in size, older machines might be easier to operate and maintain, which again suits foreign investors, given the small scale of their operations and the lack of skilled labor in the developing host countries. These factors help explain why second-hand machinery was widely used in general, and by foreign investors in particular, in LDCs, including Taiwan.

By 1969, however, imported machinery accounted for only 8.8 percent of DFI capital, and that share became negligible in the 1970s.[4]

This decline could indicate that foreign investors arriving between 1965 and 1969 used less and less old machinery, which could have happened if a large portion of DFI after 1965 was primarily export-oriented. In point of fact, DFI in Taiwan did become very export-oriented after 1965, which caused a sharp change in capital composition (this point is discussed further in section 3.4).

Second, the increasing share of reinvested earnings as a source of DFI capital reveals several important points. First, the increasing trend of that share implies the success of existing investments. More significant, as that share has increased in the 1980s to around 30 percent of the total investment, local economic conditions will have a direct bearing on the inflow of further DFI. Judging from the experience of developed countries like the United States, in which around 50 percent of DFI capital has come from retained earnings (Wichard and Freidlin 1976, p. 41), this trend of self-financing can be expected to increase.

Third, the law allows a foreign investor either to treat the technology brought in as part of the invested capital, or to license it to its subsidiary. Apparently investors prefer the latter alternative, which affords two possible advantages: (1) In licensing technology, a royalty is collected from the subsidiary, by which it is considered a cost; thus, except during the tax holiday period, there is an obvious tax incentive for licensing. (2) When technology is licensed, returns far outweigh risks.

Investor preference for licensing arrangements may change soon, however, because of the surge in high-technology industry and the establishment of a science-based industrial park in Hsing-chu, where several famous high-technology companies have organized, with no cash commitment, but capitalizing their technical know-how up to a maximum of 20 percent of the total capital (Simon and Schive 1986).

2.5 Industrial Structure of DFI in Taiwan

According to both approval and survey data, DFI in Taiwan has been concentrated heavily in the manufacturing sector. As of 1987, 89.83 percent of existing DFI was in the manufacturing sector. The electrical and electronics industry took the lion's share, accounting for 36.30 percent of the total investment; chemicals took the second-largest share, with 17.49 percent; they were followed by machinery (9.29 percent) and basic metals and metal products (8.81 percent); the other industries (garments; wood, bamboo, and rattan products; papers and paper products; etc.) accounted for a total of 14.37 percent. The service sector received only 10.17 percent of total DFI, and almost no investment took place in the primary sector (see table 7).

Because DFI in Taiwan has been dominated by non-Chinese foreigners, it should be expected that the distribution of their investment among industries is reflected in that DFI. In fact, non-Chinese investors have concentrated more on the manufacturing sector and the electrical and electronics industry than overseas Chinese have; the latter have shown a much greater tendency to invest in the service sector and the textile industry. The approval data show that 37.70 percent of total overseas Chinese investment has been in the service sector.

The differences between the industrial structures of investments by overseas Chinese and those by foreigners are attributable to the different natures of those investors. First, most overseas Chinese investors were from Hong Kong and Southeast Asia. The technological level there, except in Hong Kong, could not have been higher than that in Taiwan. As a result, their investment would concentrate naturally in the mature or light industries like textiles and nonmetallic products, mainly cements. Overseas Chinese also showed a great interest in the service sector, the construction and hotel industries in

TABLE 7   DFI BY INDUSTRY, 1987
(UNIT: PERCENT)

Industry	OVERSEAS CHINESE		NON-CHINESE		TOTAL	
	Approval (1987)	Arrival (1985)	Approval	Arrival	Approval	Arrival
Primary:	2.10	—	0.19	—	0.55	—
Manufacturing:	60.20	72.52	83.61	93.84	79.04	89.83
Textiles	6.20	15.47	0.81	1.22	1.86	3.90
Chemicals	4.07	17.44	17.35	17.51	14.76	17.49
Basic metals and products	2.66	7.18	8.09	8.41	7.03	8.18
Machinery	2.34	5.24	11.09	10.23	9.38	9.29
Electrical and electronics	3.40	5.77	35.19	43.74	28.98	36.60
Services:	37.70	27.48	16.20	6.16	20.41	10.17
Total:	100.00	100.00	100.00	100.00	100.00	100.00

SOURCES: Investment Commission, MOEA, *Statistics on Overseas Chinese and Foreign Investment, Technical Cooperation, Outward Investment, Outward Technical Cooperation,* 1987; and *An Analysis of Operations and Economic Effects of Foreign Enterprises in Taiwan,* 1985.

particular. Investment in these two industries was not generally available to most foreigners, but many overseas Chinese were allowed to invest in them after they had abandoned their claim to exchange settlement. In short, DFI from overseas Chinese represents a "neighboring" investment that differs from the more traditional, more "distant" non-Chinese DFI.

2.6 Summary

DFI in Taiwan has shown an increasing trend since 1960, with one-fifth of that investment coming from overseas Chinese, and the greatest part of the balance from the United States (31 percent), Japan (24 percent), and Europe (13 percent). Among these different investors, U.S. and European firms tended to be larger in size, and to have majority-owned capital structures; Japanese investors, on the other hand, preferred joint ventures, especially those owned nearly equally with the natives.

Prior to 1965, 50 percent of the capital introduced into Taiwan by DFI took the form of machinery, much of it very likely second-hand. Since 1965, as DFI has become more export-oriented and more profitable, a growing portion of that capital has taken the form of foreign exchange and retained earnings. The last-named source of DFI has made local economic conditions relevant to future DFI.

As regards industrial structure, non-Chinese investors have concentrated in the manufacturing sector, the electrical and electronics industry in particular. Investments by overseas Chinese have clustered in mature industries or in the service sector.

3

Technology Transfer Led by Direct Foreign Investment

Modern economic growth can be viewed as a continuous process of accumulation and application of scientific and technical knowledge (Kuznets 1966, chap. 1.6).[1] DFI is one of the most important conduits for the acquisition of that knowledge, and there are many theories of how DFI leads to international technology transfer, especially to developing countries. Because of the close relationship between DFI and technology transfer, however, it is difficult to isolate and measure the transferred technology *per se*. To overcome that difficulty and arrive at some understanding of this most interesting and complicated aspect of DFI, it will be useful to examine carefully various activities of foreign firms that have either sponsored or benefited from technology transfer.

This chapter begins by presenting theories of DFI in relation to technology transfer. Then the behaviors of foreign and national firms in applying foreign technology in manufacturing are compared. Because foreign technology can be used in developing both new products and management skills, the next two sections examine the behavior of foreign firms in introducing new products and in export marketing. In addition to DFI, foreign technology can also be acquired through licensing or technical cooperation. The next section, therefore, studies technical cooperation between foreign and Taiwanese firms. The chapter concludes with a summary.

3.1   Theories of DFI and Technology Transfer

Two approaches—the traditional trade theory and the industrial-organization theory—have been formulated to explain DFI (Johnson 1972). The traditional trade theory, though, may not be able to directly explain DFI, because the comparative-advantage doctrine that is held to guide trade may govern DFI as well.

The classical trade theory states that a country possesses comparative advantage in, and is therefore likely to export, those products that use its most abundant factors most intensively. For example, if, in comparison with its trading partners, Taiwan's labor endowment is greater than its capital, then it will have a comparative advantage in producing labor-intensive products.

Taiwan, the theory predicts, will export labor-intensive products because they accord with its comparative advantage. This prediction is based on, among other things, assumptions of identical technology and immobility of production factors across nations—assumptions that rule out DFI and technology transfer from the very beginning.

If we relax the assumption of factor immobility, and assume different rates of return for investments in different countries, then international capital flows will take place to exploit those investment opportunities. This classical version of capital movement, however, suffers from two limitations with regard to DFI: (1) It cannot explain the ever-increasing phenomenon of cross-hauling (mutual) investment that began in the 1960s between the United States and the European Economic Community (EEC), not to mention the prevailing, more complicated intraindustry phenomenon of cross-hauling investment; (2) because direct investment is not distinguished from portfolio investment, and the technological levels of all nations are still assumed to be identical, the classical version of capital movement provides no conceptual framework to deal with technology transfer as an aspect of DFI.

However, if we further relax the assumption of identical technology across nations, and assume that international technology transfer is most free within the context of a multinational company, then we find that the assumption of identical technology is valid, at least within the international network of a MNC. Under these conditions, there is an obvious incentive to invest, whether for the local market or for export, in a country that offers lower production costs. With these slight modifications, therefore, the classical wisdom can explain DFI and technology transfer and its relation to trade. In fact, many empirical studies have attributed the 1960s' surge in export-oriented DFI in the manufacturing sectors of LDCs to the significant differences in comparative advantage between the source DCs and the host LDCs (Helleiner 1973; Cohen 1975; Forre 1974).

This approach to DFI that makes use of modified classical trade theory is static in nature because it assumes that DFI takes place under stable conditions of different technological levels and resource endowments among countries. In fact, a given technology changes over time, especially for a product within a company. It is impossible, however, to predict which products will be moved ahead, or at what line stage. Vernon's product-cycle theory changes this static approach into a dynamic one (Vernon 1966).

Vernon's theory begins by analyzing a nation's comparative advantages and disadvantages in its generation of new products. A new product tends to be produced in a rich country in response to its firms' ability to develop, and its consumers' ability to purchase, the new product. High wages in the rich country allow innovators to charge a higher price for a new product and encourage labor-saving innovations. As the new product passes through the early stage of its development, its characteristics and/or the manufacturing process become standardized. As a result, the need for change declines in importance, while production costs become more crucial. If the production is not characterized by economies of scale, then the cost of labor constitutes the major difference in production costs between two countries. A company, therefore, can go abroad to exploit the cost advantage, whether for reimport or to replace domestic exports. A company may also, in order to remain competitive, be forced to follow other producers who have already become multinational.

The industrial-organization theory, developed by Hymer (1971), Kindleberger (1970), and Caves (1971 and 1974), emphasizes the competition for market shares among differentiated oligopolists. A firm may own intangible assets that can in some measure be moved from one national market to another. If these assets are knowledge that cannot be patented easily, then DFI is preferred to licensing and direct export for the fullest exploitation of the rent-yielding assets. Furthermore, the relatively large, fixed information cost required to undertake an overseas investment and develop these assets internationally favors large firms. As a result, "we expect to find direct investment in manufacturing industries marked by differentiation and fewness of sellers, or differentiated oligopoly" (Caves 1971, p. 19).

The industrial-organization approach allows two inferences about DFI in LDCs. First, product differentiation (the essence of the theory) is not affordable in LDCs, due to the limited local market and the low income level. The high tariffs and other protective schemes common in LDCs may, however, make the market attractive to investors. This type of DFI has very little to do with a country's comparative advantage.

Second, if there are cultural ties between the host and source countries, the information cost and the size of the DFI will be minimal, as evidenced in the investments of overseas Chinese and Japanese in Taiwan (see section 2.3).

After examining both the traditional trade theory and the industrial-organization approaches to DFI, it becomes clear that DFI leads to technology transfer. The first approach assumes either that the technological differential between two nations is leveled out by intracompany technology transfer; or, in the dynamic setting, that the technological change over time alters the optimal location of production by means of technology transfer.

The industrial-organization approach emphasizes that holders of advanced technology (intangible assets manifested by product differentiation, as well as managerial and marketing skills) can exploit their rent-yielding advantage to the fullest through DFI. Neither approach treats technology as a free good identical everywhere before DFI takes place. As a matter of fact, they state that it is the different levels of technology between the two countries which result in DFI.

3.2 Foreign Technology in Taiwan's Exporting Firms

In investigating whether DFI introduces new technology into the host country, we may ask a very broad question: What is the technological relationship between foreign firms and their foreign owners? In other words, when foreign parent companies have a financial stake in their subsidiaries, do they usually provide them with the technology necessary to develop and manufacture products? This same question can be asked from the subsidiaries' side: Given that "subsidiaries have potential access to the 'deep pocket' of their parents," would they be able to find the necessary technology in this "deep pocket" and, hence, to ask their parents for technical assistance? (Caves 1971, p. 16). Therefore, the hypothesis to be tested can be formulated thus: foreign firms have greater access to foreign technology, and hence adopt this technology more frequently than national firms.

A 1973 survey of 311 exporting firms in Taiwan provides the data necessary to test this hypothesis. Each firm had either minimum annual exports of $1 million or a high growth rate for exports. On the whole, foreign firms in the sample had an average export ratio of up to 90 percent, while national firms had up to 80 percent.

Table 8 reveals several distinctive findings. First of all, of 126 foreign firms, 108, or 86 percent, actually applied foreign technology in their production. By contrast, of 185 national firms only 14, or 7 percent, acquired and used foreign technology. The statistical Z value to test the difference between two mean values is overwhelmingly significant, showing that a foreign firm is far more likely to receive and use foreign technology than a national firm. Furthermore, by breaking down foreign firms into majority- and minority-owned, we also find that the controlling ownership of foreign firms affects their behavior with respect to the use of foreign technology. On the average, 90 percent of the majority-owned foreign firms used foreign technology, whereas only 64 percent of the minority-owned firms did so. Therefore, both the participation of foreign capital and the nature of a firm's controlling ownership have a great bearing on a firm's behavior in applying foreign technology.

TABLE 8   FOREIGN TECHNOLOGY IN FOREIGN AND NATIONAL EXPORTING FIRMS (UNIT: NUMBER OF FIRMS)

Industry	(1) Firms with foreign-technology participation	(2) Total number of firms	(3) (1)/(2) 100%	(4) Z value[a]
Textiles:				
(1) National firms	7	76	9	6.07**
(2) Foreign firms	13	17	76	0.44
(3) Majority-owned foreign firms[b]	8	10	80	4.46**
(4) Minority-owned foreign firms	5	7	71	
Apparel:				
(1)	2	47	4	5.75**
(2)	15	22	68	2.21**
(3)	14	18	82	1.71*
(4)	1	4	25	
Plastics and products:				
(1)	1	34	3	6.87**
(2)	24	27	89	1.13
(3)	22	24	92	3.83**
(4)	2	3	66	

TABLE 8   FOREIGN TECHNOLOGY IN FOREIGN AND NATIONAL EXPORTING FIRMS (UNIT: NUMBER OF FIRMS) *(continued)*

Industry	(1) Firms with foreign-technology participation	(2) Total number of firms	(3) (1)/(2) 100%	(4) Z value[a]
Metals and products:				
(1)	2	11	18	3.52**
(2)	13	15	87	1.63*
(3)	12	13	92	0.99
(4)	1	2	50	
Electrical and electronics				
(1)	4	17	24	5.91**
(2)	43	45	96	3.42**
(3)	38	38	100	2.16**
(4)	5	7	71	
All industries:				
(1)	14	185	8	13.83**
(2)	108	126	86	5.67**
(3)	94	103	93	7.02**
(4)	14	23	61	

SOURCE: Data were provided by Yen Hwa and Yung-sun Lee, based on a survey in fall 1972 of the manufacturing exporting firms in Taiwan conducted and sponsored jointly by the Graduate Institute of Economics, National Taiwan University, and the Kiel Institute for World Economics, West Germany.

a. Z value, the significance test of difference between two percentages, is calculated as:

$$Z = \frac{P_1 P_2}{S_{P_1 P_2}}$$

P_1, P_2: percentages of groups 1 and 2

$$S_{P_1 \cdot P_2} = [P(1-P)(N_1 + N_2)/N_1 N_2]^{1/2}$$

N_1, N_2: sample size of groups 1 and 2

$$P = (N_1 P_1 + N_2 P_2)(N_1 + N_2)$$

The first Z value refers to the test between national and foreign firms without distinguishing controlling ownership; the second, between majority-owned and minority-owned foreign firms; the third, between national and minority-owned foreign firms.

* — 1% significance level
** — 5% significance level

b. Majority-owned firms include those 50% owned.

In general, the above conclusion holds true for each individual industry. The only exceptions are: (1) in the textile industry, the minority-owned foreign firms behaved like the majority-owned ones in using foreign technology; and (2) in the metal and metal-products industry, national firms applied foreign technology as frequently as did minority-owned ones. (With regard to the latter exception, it should be noted that the sample was very small.)

In addition to the controlling ownership, the source of DFI in various foreign firms also influences the extent to which they adopt foreign technology. When most investment by overseas Chinese came from developing countries, the technological superiority generally associated with overseas-Chinese firms was not apparent. For instance, the textile and apparel industries, which were favored by overseas Chinese,[2] tended to show lower rates of participation of foreign technology than did other industries.

In short, Taiwan's case is consistent with what theories of DFI predict, namely, that foreign capital and foreign technology move hand in hand. Although the nature of the controlling ownership makes the picture slightly different, minority-owned foreign firms still receive foreign technology far more frequently than do national ones. In discussing how DFI in Taiwan is accompanied by foreign technology, however, it is important to distinguish overseas-Chinese investment from non-Chinese investment.

3.3 New Product Development

The previous section, while it indicates that foreign firms applied foreign technology more frequently than national ones, does not specify the content of that technology. In this section, *technology* will refer only to the development of new products. The data used here come from a 1976 survey of 210 firms, 68 of them foreign. The sampling process consisted of classifying firms by the commodities they produce, then randomly selecting no more than two firms to represent each commodity.[3]

The overlap in product mix among the sampled firms should, therefore, not be serious. A new producer is defined here as the first domestic producer of a particular product. Data for five major industries (auto parts, electronics and parts, plastics and plastic products, machinery, and textiles) are presented in table 9.

First of all, of 113 national firms, 42 percent have introduced new products, and 34 percent of those firms have received foreign assistance in the process. Of a total of 68 foreign firms, 54.4 percent have brought out new products, and 81 percent of those innovators have relied on foreign technology. Foreign firms, then, were only slightly more active in introducing new products, but for those that did, for-

TABLE 9   NEW PRODUCT DEVELOPMENT BY NATIONAL AND FOREIGN FIRMS

	National firms			Foreign firms		
Industry	(1) No. of firms	(2) Percent of (1) introducing new products	(3) Percent of (2) helped by foreign technology	(1)	(2)	(3)
Auto parts	11	81.8	77.7	7	85.7	100.00
Electronics and parts	30	30.0	22.2	24	62.5	93.3
Plastics and products	13	61.5	37.5	11	63.6	85.7
Machinery	41	41.5	23.5	8	25.0	50.0
Textiles	18	22.2	0	11	36.3	50.0
Total	**113**	**41.6**	**34.0**	**68**	**55.7**	**85.3**

SOURCE: Primary survey data from C. Schive et al., A Study of the Effect of Protection on Major Commodities in the Republic of China (Research, Development and Evaluation Commission, Executive Yuan, 1979) (in Chinese).

eign technology played a much more significant role than it did for national firms.

Among individual industries, a high proportion of both national and foreign makers of auto parts introduced new products (81.8 and 85.7 percent, respectively). The foreign auto-parts firms relied totally on foreign technology, while seven out of the nine national firms did so. In the electronics industry, foreign firms were far more active in developing new products and relied heavily on their parent companies for technology. The one exception to this was a joint venture to produce transistors, backed by foreign capital but with the technology coming from the laboratory of a local university. In the plastics industry, both types of firms were active in introducing new products, but foreign firms, again, were more dependent on foreign technology than were national firms.

The machinery industry reveals a different state of affairs: national firms were more innovative than foreign firms. In this industry, Taiwan, like many other developing countries, has its own machinery workshops (Leff 1968, chap. 2; Strassmann 1968, chap. 5). Advances or improvements in the technology of Taiwan's machinery industry are more likely to become apparent in the upgrading of existing products than in the development of new ones. A similar situation occurred in the textile industry, where the product line is already mature.

To sum up: Despite the crudity of the data on product innovation, some conclusions can be drawn: (1) foreign firms are not automatically product innovators, as has been the case in Taiwan's machinery and textile industries; (2) foreign firms are not always more active than national firms in introducing new products, as in the electronics and machinery industries; and (3) when foreign firms *are* product innovators, then they are much more likely than national firms to use foreign technology.

3.4 Foreign Firms and Export Marketing

This section will analyze the differences in export marketing between foreign and national firms. As was pointed out at the beginning of this study, the scope of technology includes management skills, one of the most important of which is marketing. Foreign investors with a competitive advantage in marketing (Caves 1971) tend to play an active role in the export marketing of their subsidiaries. The empirical results should firmly validate this inference.

The survey cited in section 3.2 also provides information on exporting firms' various marketing channels. Each firm was asked about its sources of information on foreign marketing, including: (1) its foreign partners; (2) foreign agents; (3) foreign customers; (4) government agents or industrial associations; (5) trading companies; and (6) international fairs. The results are presented in table 10.

A significant finding shown in table 10 is that a large proportion (86 percent) of national firms received export-market information from their foreign customers. The same situation also holds true for foreign firms. After those foreign firms are eliminated whose marketing was handled exclusively by their foreign owners, 84.0 percent of the remaining foreign firms had the same major export-marketing strategy as national firms.

Of a total of 127 foreign exporting firms, 95 (74.8 percent) utilized their parent companies' facilities for export marketing, either exclusively or in conjunction with other marketing methods. The proportion of majority-owned foreign firms whose marketing was handled by parents went up to 80 percent. Further examination of the data shows that 26 (20.5 percent) of the foreign firms relied completely on this marketing method, which was available only to foreign firms. Of those 26 foreign firms, 25 were majority-owned, and 11 were in the

TABLE 10   EXPORT MARKETING METHODS OF TAIWAN'S EXPORTING FOREIGN AND NATIONAL FIRMS, BY INDUSTRY (UNIT: PERCENT)

Industry	Number of firms	Foreign agents	International fairs	Foreign customers	Foreign partners	Industrial associations	Trading companies
Textiles:							
(1) National firms	76	22.4	7.9	85.5	—	46.1	19.7
(2) Foreign firms	17	53.0	17.6	52.9	47.1	35.5	5.9
(3) Majority-owned foreign firms	10	40.0	30.0	40.0	50.0	40.0	—
(4) Minority-owned foreign firms	7	71.4	—	71.4	42.9	28.6	14.3
Apparel:							
(1)	49	32.7	12.2	87.8	—	26.5	14.3
(2)	22	40.9	9.1	72.7	81.8	4.5	9.1
(3)	18	44.4	5.6	66.7	88.9	5.6	5.6
(4)	4	25.0	25.0	100.0	50.0	—	25.0
Plastic and products:							
(1)	34	35.3	11.8	94.1	—	26.5	8.8
(2)	27	37.0	14.8	70.4	74.1	18.5	7.4
(3)	24	33.3	12.5	70.8	75.0	16.7	4.2
(4)	3	66.7	33.3	66.7	66.7	33.3	33.3
Metal products:							
(1)	11	54.5	27.3	81.8	—	36.4	9.1
(2)	15	6.7	—	80.0	80.0	—	—
(3)	13	7.7	—	76.9	84.6	—	—
(4)	2	—	—	100.0	50.0	—	—
Electrical and electronics:							
(1)	17	29.4	17.6	76.5	—	47.1	—
(2)	46	50.0	15.2	63.0	80.4	19.6	—
(3)	39	51.3	12.8	56.4	87.2	17.9	—
(4)	7	42.9	28.6	100.0	42.9	28.6	—
All industries:							
(1)	187	29.9	11.8	86.6	—	36.9	13.9
(2)	127	40.9	12.6	66.9	74.8	16.5	3.9
(3)	104	39.4	11.5	62.5	80.8	15.4	1.9
(4)	23	47.8	17.4	87.0	47.8	21.7	13.0

SOURCE: Same as for table 8.
NOTE: Each firm may use more than one marketing method at any given time.

electrical and electronics industry. In general, marketing through foreign firms was the most popular of the six export-marketing methods
available to foreign firms. We can conclude that, in addition to introducing technology, DFI has alleviated Taiwan's export-marketing
problems, and has helped promote effective exportation of its products.

Foreign investors take charge of exporting their subsidiaries' products for several reasons besides market familiarity. First, vertical inte-
gration exists in the manufacturing sector; exporting semifinished
products for final assembly in another country is common among
multinational corporations. Second, for those products requiring
after-sale service, parent companies' marketing and service networks
are advantageous to foreign firms. Finally, if a transfer price policy is
to be enforced, a parent company must take over its subsidiary's export operation (Hanson 1975).[4] All these facts have one important implication: if a parent company is in full charge of its subsidiary's
marketing, then that subsidiary's exports can increase greatly within a
relatively short period.

The limited data for the electrical and electronics industry support
this argument. The 11 foreign firms in that industry whose exports
were handled entirely by their parents had average exports of $11.7
million in 1972. The other 28 majority-owned foreign firms in the
same industry had average exports of only $5.1 million. Eight of those
11 exporting foreign firms were established after 1968. Their parents'
assistance in export marketing must have played a decisive role in
helping them achieve so huge a volume of exports within the brief
span of four years from 1968 to 1972.

As for other channels of marketing information, foreign firms obtained market information more frequently from foreign agents and
international fairs than did national firms. Foreign firms, with the help
of their foreign owners, found it easier to line up foreign agents or to
attend international trade fairs. National firms, on the other hand, relied more on trading companies and industrial associations, as would
be expected.

The parent companies of majority-owned foreign firms tended to
take a more active role in their subsidiaries' export marketing. On the
other hand, foreign customers and trading companies seem to have
played a larger part in the export marketing of minority-owned firms
than of majority-owned ones. National firms behaved much the same
as did minority-owned foreign firms, except that the latter still had a
significant tendency to involve their foreign partners in their export
operations. Thus, on the one hand, minority- and majority-owned
foreign firms both tended to exploit their foreign owners' marketing

facilities; on the other hand, minority-owned foreign firms behaved identically to national firms in export marketing, except that the foreign firms had an advantage over national firms in their access to their foreign owners' marketing facilities.

In general, the above findings hold true for each individual industry. A more detailed discriminant-function analysis providing statistical validation of the above findings is presented in the addendum to this chapter.

To sum up: DFI by a parent company not only alleviates its subsidiary's technology constraints, but also solves its problem of unfamiliarity with the export market. The immediate effect is that a large-scale subsidiary can be set up without marketing constraints. Because of the foreign ties foreign partners provide, foreign firms have been more active in attending foreign trade fairs and in cultivating foreign agents, while domestic firms have relied more on industrial associations and trading companies. The behavior of minority-owned foreign firms has included characteristics of the behaviors of both majority-owned foreign firms and national firms.

3.5 Foreign Firms and Technical Cooperation

Under the existing Statute of Technical Cooperation, local firms are permitted to acquire technical know-how from abroad for the following purposes: (1) introducing a new product; (2) increasing production, improving quality, or reducing costs; and (3) providing management skills, or acquiring designs, processing techniques, or patents. In the previous sections of this chapter, foreign firms were found to have maintained close technological ties with their parent companies or foreign partners. Chapter Two, however, showed that very few foreign companies in Taiwan have capitalized their technology as part of their initial capital. Foreign firms must, accordingly, use the channel of contracted technical cooperation to transfer technology whenever possible. An examination of data on technical cooperation will be useful in understanding the content, motivations, and terms of such contracts as are made by foreign firms.

First of all, the industrial distribution of technical cooperation did not change over the ten-year period from 1975 to 1986. Four industries (electrical and electronics, machinery, chemicals, and basic metals) accounted for around 75 percent and 73 percent of all contracts for technical cooperation in 1975 and 1986, respectively (see table 11).

TABLE 11   TECHNICAL COOPERATION BY INDUSTRY, 1975 AND 1986
             (UNITS: CASES, PERCENT)

	1975		1986	
Industry	*Cases*	*Percent*	*Cases*	*Percent*
Foods and beverages	15	3.16	87	3.58
Textiles	22	4.64	62	2.55
Apparel	4	0.84	24	0.99
Paper and products	10	2.11	27	1.11
Rubber and plastic products	22	4.64	137	5.64
Chemicals	76	16.03	487	20.07
Nonmetallic products	18	3.80	92	3.79
Primary metals	64	13.50	288	11.87
Machinery	76	16.03	362	14.91
Electrical and electronics	141	29.75	633	26.08
Construction	9	1.90	27	1.11
Services	10	2.11	104	4.29
Other	7	1.48	83	3.42
All industries	**474**	**100.0**	**2,427**	**99.41**

SOURCE: Investment Commission, MOEA, *Statistics on Overseas Chinese and Foreign Investment, Technical Cooperation, Outward Investment and Outward Technical Cooperation in the Republic of China,* 1976 and 1986.
NOTE: 1986 data cover technical cooperation in several industries not listed here.

In 1975, there were a total of 451 valid technical-cooperation contracts between local companies and licensers of foreign technology, with 134, or 29.7 percent, of them granted to foreign firms. A large proportion (73.1 percent) of the latter contracts were signed between foreign firms and their foreign investors. The percentage is even higher (84.9 percent) in the electrical and electronics industry. These percentages may be underestimated, because foreign technology is sometimes provided by unidentified affiliates of foreign investors. Thus, foreign firms did not exclusively use this special channel to transfer technology (see table 12).

There are several potential benefits from treating imported technology as technical cooperation rather than as capital. The first two benefits have been mentioned above: (1) remitted royalties and fees are taxed only once, as foreign income, while remitted profits are taxed as both corporate and foreign income (except during the tax hol-

TABLE 12   TECHNICAL COOPERATION BY INDUSTRY AND BY SOURCE COUNTRY, 1975
(UNIT: NUMBER OF CASES)

Industry	United States			Japan			Europe and Others			All Foreign Firms		
	(1) Signed by foreign firms	(2) Signed between foreign firms and their foreign owners	(3) Total	(1)	(2)	(3)	(1)	(2)	(3)	(1)	(2)	(3)
Foods and beverages	1	1	4	—	—	10	—	—	1	1	1	15
Textiles	2	—	11	1	—	10	—	—	1	3	0	22
Apparel	—	—	3	1	1	1	—	—	—	1	1	4
Paper and products	—	—	4	—	—	5	—	—	1	—	—	10
Rubber and plastic products	2	2	4	3	2	16	1	—	2	6	4	22
Chemicals	10	6	26	5	4	34	4	2	16	19	12	76
Nonmetallic products	—	—	4	2	2	11	—	—	3	2	2	18
Primary metal and metal products	2	2	10	12	4	48	—	—	6	14	6	64
Machinery	3	1	11	11	9	58	1	—	7	15	10	76
Electrical and electronics	20	17	40	48	41	97	5	4	7	73	62	144
All industries	**40**	**29**	**117**	**83**	**63**	**290**	**11**	**6**	**44**	**134**	**98**	**451**

SOURCE: Primary data from Investment Commission, MOEA.
NOTE: All technical cooperations presented were actual cases as of the end of 1975.

iday period); and (2) royalties and fees are paid when production begins, which is not the case for profits. The third benefit from treating transferred technology as technical cooperation is that, if that technology is also patented, the R&D section of the parent company may prefer to license it for cash income. Finally, the licensing of a company's technology to its own subsidiary is not an arm's-length transaction: the parent company may reap further advantages from this situation.

In order to verify this last point, it is necessary to examine and compare the terms of contracts for technical cooperation made by foreign and national firms. In general, royalties are charged on a percentage of net sales (sales minus materials provided by licenser) for some given period. The average for these two figures in typical technical-cooperation contracts approved in 1971–1975 were 3 percent and 5 years. Table 13 presents these data for national firms and for foreign firms whose licensers were also investors.

TABLE 13   COOPERATION PERIOD AND RATES OF RETURN OF TECHNICAL COOPERATIONS, BY NATIONAL AND FOREIGN FIRMS, SELECTED INDUSTRIES
(UNITS: COOPERATION PERIODS, YEARS; RATES OF RETURN, PERCENT)

| | Foreign firms | | | | National firms | |
| | Majority-owned | | Minority-owned | | | |
Industry	Cooperation period	Rate of return	Cooperation period	Rate of return	Cooperation period	Rate of return
Electrical and electronics	5.4 (27)	3.10 (24)	4.8 (18)	2.13 (16)	4.9 (64)	3.05 (56)
Chemicals	4.4 (13)	3.75 (9)	5.0 (1)	5.00 (1)	6.1 (55)	3.35 (32)
Machinery	5.8 (4)	2.25 (4)	4.0 (1)	4.00 (1)	5.9 (48)	3.54 (48)
Metal products	5.0 (3)	1.83 (3)	4.0 (2)	3.80 (2)	5.6 (45)	3.40 (30)

SOURCE: Primary data from Investment Commission, MOEA.
NOTE: Technical cooperations presented were limited to those signed during the period of 1971–1975. Figures in parentheses represent the number of cases of technical cooperation observed. Technical cooperation agreements signed by foreign firms were defined as intra-company technology transfers. In a few cases, royalties were paid in a lump sum, and hence cannot be converted into percentage figures.

We can make a few observations. First, majority-owned firms in the electrical and electronics industry tended to sign longer-term and higher-paid contracts with their foreign technology holders, most likely their parent companies, than did minority-owned foreign firms and national firms. In fact, the latter two groups behave almost identically, which suggests that, beyond a certain point, foreign ownership did affect bargaining positions and, thus, contract terms.

The situation is different for the other three industries, where majority-owned foreign firms had shorter cooperation periods and lower royalties. (It should be noted, however, that the sample sizes for these three groups, especially for the machinery and basic metals industries, are relatively small.) Based on the data from the electrical and electronics industry, though, we are probably safe in concluding that foreign investors did, to some extent, exercise their privilege of raising the rent on their intangible assets.

That conclusion raises the question: Can the "exploitation" of a host country by an MNC be prohibited? The main difficulty is the practical one of identifying similar technologies for which different rates are being charged. The Investment Commission did have a screening process to reduce that probability without causing applicants needless trouble. Applications for technical cooperation in manufacturing were sent to the Industrial Technology and Research Institution, a government-sponsored research center, for evaluation. Because Taiwan was anxious to acquire foreign technology, few applications were rejected, but the process did focus attention on contract terms. In cases where similar technologies were being introduced at higher royalty scales and/or for longer terms than their counterparts elsewhere, applicants were required to provide justification, such as the terms obtained in other countries. This process, intended to control abnormal cases, has gained support from both minority-owned foreign firms and national firms.

Another loophole that may be used by foreign investors consists in extending the cooperation period beyond its expiration. The existing data show that 32 (38.6 percent) of the 83 contracts renewed in 1971–1975 were intracompany contracts. In the context of all technical-cooperation contracts attributable to intracompany agreements, 21.7 percent of foreign firms prolonged their cooperation periods. The data show, however, that most renewal cases were deemed necessary, either for patent protection or to acquire improved, more advanced technology. That consideration, therefore, should moderate any conclusions reached on the basis of these figures.

In seeking to compare Taiwan's royalty payments with those of other countries, we find that Australia's royalties amounted to around

3 percent of sales in the 1970s (Parry and Watson 1979). Data from UN-IDO (United Nations Industrial Development Organization) show that royalties of 5 percent of sales are common (Moxon 1979). In India, the average royalty fee as a percentage of sales was reduced from 4.25 percent in 1951 to 2.0 percent in 1967, but this has hindered India's long-term technological development (Davis 1977). On the basis of these incomplete data and those presented in table 13, it may be concluded that Taiwan's royalty payments were about average, although parent companies of foreign firms might sometimes charge a slightly higher rate than national firms for their technology. Unfortunately, our data do not allow us to decide whether that difference was due to the superiority of the technology associated with foreign firms.

3.6 Summary

Theories of DFI suggest that it is an efficient channel of international technology migration. Empirical study of foreign firms' behavior in Taiwan reveals that the participation of foreign capital in them did indeed lead to their use of foreign technology. As to the specific technologies imported through DFI, foreign firms played an important role in introducing new products and technologies in the auto and auto-parts, electrical and electronics, and plastic and plastic-products industries, but they were less active in the machinery and textile industries.

We find also that foreign investors are very likely to use their worldwide marketing networks to handle their subsidiaries' export marketing, either exclusively or at least in part. The empirical results show that 74.8 percent of exporting foreign firms relied at least partially on their foreign owners for their export marketing. Foreign subsidiaries can be set up on a larger scale from the outset when they do not face export-marketing constraints. Finally, DFI has tried to win various concessions in applying for permission for technical cooperation; one of the most crucial areas has been contract terms. The empirical results show that majority-owned foreign firms in the electrical and electronics industry signed slightly longer-term and somewhat more expensive contracts for their parent companies' technologies than did national or even minority-owned firms. The slightness of the differences between majority-owned foreign firms and the other two types precludes any firm conclusion that the parent companies of the former have demanded more control when granting access to their technologies.

3.7 Addendum: A Discriminant-function Analysis of Foreign Firms' Export Marketing

The discriminant-function technique is similar to the single-equation regression model, except that the dependent variable is a dummy variable. The basic aim of the discriminant-function technique is to find out which explanatory variable can best discriminate the dependent dummy variable, which in this case represents a foreign or national firm. The explanatory variables refer to the six different marketing methods firms may adopt. In setting up a model, we assume:

$Y_i = 1$, if the ith firm is a foreign firm (in different cases, Y_i will refer to majority- or minority-owned firms)

$= 0$, elsewhere

$X_{ij} = 1$, if the ith firm adopted the jth marketing method:

   $j = 1$: marketing through foreign agents
   $j = 2$: marketing through attending international fairs
   $j = 3$: marketing through foreign customers
   $j = 4$: marketing through foreign owners
   $j = 5$: marketing through government agents and/or industrial associations
   $j = 6$: marketing through trading companies
   $j = 0$: elsewhere

We then estimate:

$Y_i = b_0 + \Sigma_j b_j X_{ij}$

The results do not change the general conclusions reached in this chapter, except that: (1) In the textile industry, national firms were more interested than foreign firms in marketing directly to their foreign customers; (2) In the apparel and plastic and plastic-products industries, foreign firms were more active than national firms in approaching government agents or trading companies (see table 14).

TABLE 14   DISCRIMINANT-FUNCTION ANALYSIS OF EXPORT MARKETING BEHAVIOR BETWEEN NATIONAL AND FOREIGN FIRMS

Industry	Discriminating variables	b	Marginal F value	Cumulative F value
All industries:				
Y = 1, foreign firm	X_4	.8447	270.69**	270.69**
0, national firm	X_1	.0882	10.46**	189.46**
	X_2	.1841	10.14**	148.78**
	X_5	−.0422	1.18	119.33**
	X_3	−.0382	.82	99.51**
	X_6	.0126	.09	85.31**
Foreign firms:				
Y = 1, majority-owned	X_4	.2297	5.64**	5.64**
0, minority-owned	X_3	−.1515	4.89**	5.48**
	X_6	−.2956	2.69*	4.84**
	X_5	.0669	.68	4.00**
	X_2	.0392	.09	3.32**
	X_1	−.0203	.07	2.83**
National vs. minority-owned foreign firms:				
Y = 1, minority-owned foreign firm	X_4	.9285	92.62**	92.62**
0, national firm	X_1	.0475	2.22	62.83**
	X_2	.0674	1.23	47.48**
	X_5	−.0366	1.15	41.20**
	X_3	.0306	.36	31.88**
	X_6	.0216	.20	27.25**
Textiles:				
Y = 1, foreign firm	X_4	.7968	26.03**	26.03**
0, national firm	X_3	−.1490	3.84**	19.17**
	X_2	.2294	3.42**	16.22**
	X_1	.1052	2.91*	13.83**
	X_6	.0953	.84	11.65**
	X_5	−.0591	.84	10.08**

SOURCE: Same as for table 4.
NOTE: * — F value significant at the 5% level
    ** — F value significant at the 1% level
a. No firm adopted the X_6 marketing method.

TABLE 14   DISCRIMINANT-FUNCTION ANALYSIS OF EXPORT MARKETING BEHAVIOR
BETWEEN NATIONAL AND FOREIGN FIRMS *(continued)*

Industry	Discriminating variables	b	Marginal F value	Cumulative F value
Apparel:				
Y = 1, foreign firm	X_4	.9856	107.14**	107.14**
0, national firm	X_2	.2360	5.72**	78.22**
	X_6	.2082	5.59**	63.98**
	X_5	−.0662	1.07	51.47**
	X_1	.0632	1.07	43.13**
	X_3	.0489	.45	36.71**
Plastic and products:				
Y = 1, foreign firm	X_4	.9274	46.98**	46.98**
0, national firm	X_2	.3496	13.22**	42.21**
	X_5	.1618	2.70*	33.27**
	X_3	−.1423	2.15	27.58**
	X_6	.1294	.99	23.14**
	X_1	−.0161	.02	19.49**
Metal products:[a]				
Y = 1, foreign firm	X_4	.7111	33.00**	33.00**
0, national firm	X_5	−.2000	2.03	23.61**
	X_3	.1489	1.14	18.11**
	X_1	−.0244	.04	13.59**
	X_2	−.0252	.01	11.00**
Electrical and electronics:[a]				
Y = 1, foreign firm	X_4	.6110	33.84**	33.84**
0, national firm	X_1	.1033	1.61	23.32**
	X_5	−.1278	.74	17.59**
	X_2	.1008	.68	14.14**
	X_3	−.0435	.24	11.67**

SOURCE: Same as for table 4.
NOTES: *   — F value significant at the 5% level
　　　** — F value significant at the 1% level
a. No firm adopted the X_6 marketing method.

4

Foreign Firms' Technology, Employment, and Exports

When introducing a new technology into its production process, whether to make a new product or to introduce a new process, or whether it takes the form of improved equipment or different organizational structure, a firm must carefully evaluate the different aspects of that technology in order to ensure that the best results can be obtained from it.[1] In the neoclassical framework, the issue, related to DFI, is how, or to what extent, imported technology affects the efficiency of resource allocation. Given the abundance of labor and the shortage of capital in an LDC, "appropriate" technology will be labor-intensive—employment as a function of capital committed will be maximized—as a response to either the low cost of labor or the high cost of capital. The essential question remains, however, whether the technology brought into an LDC economy through DFI will be "appropriate."

There have been two alternative hypotheses regarding technology. The first states that if foreign firms apply the same technology as their parent companies (presumably capital-intensive, given the relatively low capital cost and relatively high wages in DCs as compared to LDCs), then DFI will decrease the efficiency of resource allocation.

The second hypothesis says that, because of foreign firms' advantages in technology, access to information, or simply experience, they may have more options in choosing technologies or in adapting them to their host countries' needs. Thus, they will improve resource allocation in their host countries by applying more suitable technologies than do their counterparts.

Our empirical findings must decide which of these conflicting hypotheses is correct.

This chapter will use the available data to compare the factor proportions (*i.e.*, various measures of the capital-labor ratio) of foreign and national firms in Taiwan. The first section will concentrate on a comparison of these two types of firms at the national level, taking the industrial distribution of investment into account. A comparison over a narrowly defined industry base will be made in section 2. Section 3 will focus on comparison of foreign firms with distinctive market orientations—those aiming at export or local markets. Finally, some conclusions will be drawn from these comparisons.[2]

4.1 An Overall Comparison Between Foreign and National Firms' Factor Intensities

The data for this part of the study are provided by two surveys: the foreign-firm survey and the 1976 census. The census data, which included all foreign and national firms, were classified for purposes of comparison into twelve industries, ignoring the size and product mix of the firms.

Table 15 shows that in 1976 foreign firms, on the whole, used an average of $6,490 in fixed assets per employee, compared with $7,150 for national firms. Foreign firms used more labor-intensive technologies than national firms in producing foods and beverages, apparel, wood, bamboo, and rattan products, leather products, rubber and plastic products, chemicals, and electrical and electronic products. In the textile, paper-products, nonmetallic-products, and machinery industries, however, foreign firms used more capital-intensive technologies than their local counterparts. The nonmetallic-products industry is an extreme case: in that industry foreign firms had a very high capital-labor ratio compared not only with national firms in the same industry, but also with foreign firms in other industries. A careful examination of foreign firms in the nonmetallic industry reveals that a few large minority-owned foreign cement factories accounted for that high capital-labor ratio. Indeed, foreign firms' capital intensities varied among industries, and did not exhibit any consistent pattern in relation to the capital intensities of local firms in the same industries.

The above findings suggest that, in order to explain the differences in factor intensity between national and foreign firms, the in-

TABLE 15   FIXED ASSETS PER EMPLOYEE OF NATIONAL AND FOREIGN
MANUFACTURING FIRMS, BY INDUSTRY, 1976[a]
(UNIT: $1,000)

| | Foreign Firms | | | National |
Industry	Overseas Chinese	Non-Chinese	Total	Firms
Foods and beverages	4.32	6.13	5.10	11.68
Textiles	10.29	25.66	17.74	7.61
Apparel	1.32	1.13	1.24	1.53
Wood, bamboo, and rattan products	3.79	1.87	2.79	3.87
Paper and products	12.13	9.58	10.92	6.89
Feather and leather products	1.63	0.97	1.32	1.74
Rubber and plastic products	2.29	2.05	2.13	3.58
Chemicals	15.05	11.66	13.32	21.84
Nonmetallic products	33.13	22.21	27.53	7.39
Basic metals and products	1.74	4.42	3.79	9.42
Machinery	1.74	17.32	16.32	6.87
Electrical and electronics	2.58	2.60	2.60	4.55
Manufacturing, total[b]	**8.20**	**5.77**	**6.49**	**7.15**

SOURCES: Investment Commission, MOEA, *An Analysis of Operations and Economic Effects of Foreign Enterprise* (Taipei, 1977); *The Report of 1976, the Committee on Industrial and Commercial Censuses of Taiwan-Fukien District of the Republic of China* (Taipei, 1978).
NOTES:
a. Figures were weighted averages.
b. The figure for the national manufacturing total including some industries with no DFI, such as the refinery and miscellaneous industries, was $8,390.

dustrial structures of both types of investment should be taken into account. Since the average capital-labor ratio (k) is a weighted average of each individual industry's capital-labor ratio (k_i) by employment (w_i), the difference between the averages k_f, representing foreign firms, and k_n, representing national firms, can be decomposed into two parts. One of these parts is attributable to the difference in k_i (the ith industry's capital-labor ratio) between foreign and national firms; the other is attributable to the difference in w_i (the industrial structure measured by employment) between foreign and national firms. The first part of the deviation is due to intraindustry differences in k; the second part is due to interindustry differences in distribution. In other words, the use by foreign firms, as a whole, of more (or less) capital-intensive technology may have been due to one or both of two factors; for in each individual industry, foreign firms used more (or less) capital-intensive technology than did their national counterparts and foreign firms were more (or less) concentrated in capital-intensive industries. These two factors need not have the same direction of influence.

The results in table 16 indicate that, on the basis of the employment structures of both national and foreign firms, foreign firms used more capital-intensive technology than did national ones, on the average. However, because DFI has tended to be concentrated in more labor-intensive industries, foreign firms, on the whole, also tended to use more labor-intensive technology, though the intraindustry comparison shows different results. Thus it is not the intraindustry difference in factor intensity, but the difference in investment structure, between national and foreign firms, that governs and explains the overall difference in factor intensities between these two groups: whether a foreign firm adopted a more capital-intensive technology than a national one in a given industry may not have been as important as the firm's choice of industry for the determination of its overall technological characteristics.

4.2 Comparison of Foreign and National Firms' Factor Intensities by Industry

So far, our comparison has been made at a highly aggregated level. Similar studies can be carried out within much more narrowly defined industries. The data used for comparison were derived from a survey of national and foreign firms of similar size producing similar goods (see section 3.3) and from a sample from the 1976 census using the same criteria. Table 17 presents several measures of factor intensity for foreign and national manufacturers in the artificial fiber and the TV and TV-parts industries. The four foreign artificial fiber companies used more capital-intensive technology than did national companies, as measured both in fixed assets per employee and in machinery and equipment costs per worker; this difference, however, was not statistically significant. Foreign and national firms paid nearly the same electricity cost per worker.

In the TV and parts industry, national firms applied more capital-intensive technology in terms of machinery and equipment per worker than foreign firms did, which seems to contradict the findings in table 15 for the electrical and electronics industry. Measured in

TABLE 16   DIFFERENCES IN FACTOR INTENSITY BETWEEN NATIONAL AND FOREIGN
FIRMS DUE TO INTRA- AND INTERINDUSTRY DIFFERENCES
(UNIT: $1,000 PER EMPLOYEE)

	Total difference of **k** (national firms minus foreign firms)	Intraindustry difference	Interindustry difference
Based on national firm's employment structure	0.66	−2.41 (−365.15)	3.07 (465.15)
Based on foreign firm's employment structure	0.66	−0.16 (−24.24)	0.82 (124.24)

SOURCES: Same as those for table 15.
NOTE: Decomposing formula derived as follows:

$$k^N - k^f = \sum k_i^N w_i^N - k_i^f w_i^f$$
$$= \sum (k_i^N - k_i^f) w_i^N + \sum (w_i^N - w_i^n) k_i^f$$
$$= \sum (k_i^N - k_i^f) w_i^f + \sum (w_i^N - w_i^f) k_i^N$$

N = national; f = foreign; k = fixed assets per employee; w = employment share; i = "i"th industry.

TABLE 17   CAPITAL-LABOR RATIOS OF FOREIGN AND NATIONAL FIRMS:
ARTIFICIAL FIBER AND TV AND PARTS INDUSTRIES, 1976
(UNIT: $1,000)

	Artificial Fiber			TV and TV-Parts		
	Foreign	National	t	Foreign	National	t
Number of firms	4.00	20.00	0.71	33.00	41.00	—
Fixed assets per employee	58.29	42.50	0.71	3.34	2.32	1.46
Machinery and equipment per employee	68.66	55.68	0.66	2.76	3.39	−0.83
Electricity cost per employee	1.71	1.76	0.09	0.13	0.14	−0.21

SOURCE: Primary data from Schive and Yeh 1980.

TABLE 18 CAPITAL-LABOR RATIOS OF FOREIGN AND NATIONAL FIRMS: PLASTIC AND PRODUCTS, AUTO PARTS, AND ELECTRONICS INDUSTRIES, 1974
(UNIT: $1,000)

	Plastic and Products			Auto Parts			Electronics		
	Foreign	National	t	Foreign	National	t	Foreign	National	t
Number of firms	6	9		5	8		16	20	
Average number of employees	263	325		169	87		871	532	
Average sales	6,513	5,679	0.39	1,227	678	-0.20	8,710	6,748	-0.85
Fixed assets per employee	3.03	2.89	0.11	5.87	2.24	1.27	1.84	1.92	-0.12

SOURCE: Primary data from Schive et al. 1978

fixed assets per employee, however, foreign firms used more capital. None of these differences was significant, however. Taking electricity cost per worker as another measure of capital intensity, the technologies of both groups of firms were similar.

Table 18 presents capital-labor ratios for the plastics and plastic-products, auto-parts, and electronics industries in 1974. In the plastics and plastic-products industry, firms in both groups that had similar employment and sales showed little difference in fixed assets per employee. This result contradicts Riedel's finding that foreign firms' technology in this industry was more labor-intensive (Riedel 1975).[3]

In the auto-parts industry (a subsector of the broadly defined machinery industry), foreign firms were more capital-intensive than national ones, which is consistent with the finding presented in table 15. Finally, in the electronics industry, both types of firms applied similar technology and paid the same costs in terms of fixed assets per employee. This result deviates from the finding in table 15, but the data presented here were limited strictly to electronics manufacturers, and excluded manufacturers of electrical equipment like cable and wire, which belong to heavy industry, and of which there are no foreign producers.

It becomes apparent that, while foreign and national firms' capital intensities may be different when compared at a higher level of aggregation, they prove to be more similar when industries are more narrowly defined. The considerable difference in the behavior of foreign and national firms in terms of factor proportions in certain industries, as shown in table 15, is most likely attributable to their different product mixes, rather than to different capital-labor ratios for similar products. If this inference is correct, more emphasis should be given to which industries DFI enters and to which products foreign firms produce, than to whether those firms apply more capital-intensive technologies for their specific products.

4.3 Factor Intensity of Foreign Firms with Different Market Orientations

Although direct comparison of national and foreign firms' technologies within the same industry shows no significant differences, similar studies of foreign firms with respect to their different market orientations may show other results. The data used for this comparison—the most comprehensive data available so far—are from the annual survey of foreign firms conducted by the Investment Commission of the Ministry of Economic Affairs. The sample comprises 749 foreign firms in Taiwan in 1975. Each firm's capital-labor ratio was weighted by its export activity; for this purpose, it was assumed that each firm used identical technology for the products it exported, and the products it sold domestically. Two measures of capital intensity (machinery and equipment per unit of direct labor, and fixed assets per employee) are presented in table 19.

On the average, foreign manufacturing firms used $7,600 worth of machinery and equipment per unit of labor in export activities, but $15,500 in production for the domestic market. As to the value of fixed assets per employee, foreign firms used half as much capital per unit

TABLE 19   CAPITAL-LABOR RATIOS OF FOREIGN FIRMS, WEIGHTED BY EXPORT
AND DOMESTIC SALES, BY INDUSTRY, 1975
(UNIT: $1,000)

Industry	Machinery and equip. per direct labor		Fixed assets per employee		Exports/sales (percent)
	Exports	Domestic sales	Exports	Domestic sales	
Foods and beverages	1.92	8.45	3.11	12.26	20.77
Textiles	21.24	14.34	26.84	19.95	77.61
Apparel	0.63	1.47	1.26	2.34	96.84
Wood, bamboo, and rattan products	1.18	1.37	1.92	2.74	93.89
Paper and products	8.74	8.87	12.00	11.42	16.69
Leather and products	0.66	1.63	1.61	2.76	99.96
Plastic and rubber products	1.42	13.03	2.29	10.76	85.29
Chemicals	17.55	19.61	16.24	17.61	43.17
Nonmetallic products	28.71	42.97	24.58	50.79	8.58
Basic metals and products	2.42	4.08	3.89	5.24	50.13
Machinery	2.08	9.45	3.32	10.47	35.67
Electrical and electronics	2.05	1.95	2.89	3.95	63.56
Total	**7.55**	**15.47**	**9.00**	**18.18**	**57.96**

SOURCE: Primary data from foreign-firm survey conducted by the Investment Commission, MOEA, 1975.

of labor in export-oriented production as they did in production for the local market. Apparently, foreign firms as a whole tended to use different technologies for different markets.

In the industries producing foods and beverages, apparel, plastic and rubber products, nonmetallic products, and machinery, foreign firms used much more capital-intensive technology for domestic sales than for exports. Foreign firms producing wood, bamboo, and rattan products, and paper and paper products applied much the same technology for both markets. The only anomaly is the textile industry, in which firms used more capital-intensive technology for exports than for the domestic market. A close examination of the data reveals that a few major producers of artificial fibers were highly export-oriented and used capital-intensive technology. Foreign firms in the wood, bamboo, and rattan industry had a very high export ratio for that year (93.89 percent), while those in the paper and paper products industry exported only 16.69 percent of their production. The former industry, therefore, was very export-oriented, while the latter targeted the local market. This one-sided market orientation and the considerable homogeneity of the product invalidate any correlation between the market orientations and technologies used by foreign firms in these two industries.

The finding for the electrical and electronics industry is unusual: in their production for export, foreign firms used slightly more capital-intensive technology than they did in their production for the local market, in terms of machinery and equipment per unit of direct labor. That situation is reversed, however, when we measure the capital-labor ratio in terms of fixed assets per employee. This disparity may stem from two factors. First, this industry has a very broad scope of production, ranging from heavy electrical equipment to home appliances to electronics and parts. The manufacture of some products, for instance, electrical equipment and electronic parts, requires heavy capital commitment. Many parts producers came to Taiwan expressly because of the strong local demand that exports had created, as evidenced by the high proportion of indirect exports (products sold to downstream processors for export; see table A-2) to total sales. Thus, some of the exports in this industry may be capital-intensive by nature. The second factor relates to an assumption we made at the beginning: the technologies for the export and domestic markets may, in fact, *not* be identical within the same company. Nonetheless, product mixes tend to average out the different characteristics of the technologies associated with different products.

The examination of a group of foreign firms located in EPZs which exported all their production and seemed not to have a broad scope of production, sheds some light on the above arguments. Foreign electrical and electronics producers in EPZs had only $789 worth of machinery per unit of labor—38.46 percent of the overall average for that industry. Thus, the highly export-oriented foreign firms, as represented by foreign firms in EPZs, used even more labor-intensive technology than did firms producing for mixed markets.

The EPZ data also help us understand why production-line technologies, as measured by the value of machinery and equipment per unit of direct labor, do not differ with respect to their varying market destinations, while overall technological levels are different for different buyers. When the marketing of an export-oriented foreign firm is taken care of by its parent company, many investments linked to marketing become unnecessary. Such investments include overhead costs of the headquarters' office, inventory, and distribution-channel costs. Their absence will be reflected in a high materials-to-sales ratio, or in the low value-added ratio, for firms that are wholly export-oriented. In the electrical and electronics industry, foreign firms in EPZs had materials-to-sales ratios of 78.07 percent, as compared to a 53.98 percent figure for foreign firms outside EPZs (see table 20). Consequently, it is logical that the same group of firms may have different technological levels, depending on their market strategies.

4.4 Effect of Technology Differences in Employment

Returning to the question of resource allocation, foreign firms that apply labor-intensive technology in their production for export must have a significant effect on local employment. Two indicators will illustrate this point clearly. First, assuming identical employment per dollar of sales, we may separate employment due to production for export from that for local sales by using the sales data for the two markets. Summing these figures for each industry and dividing the total for a given industry by its total employment will indicate the industry-level employment effects attributable to exports and to domestic sales.

If the total percentage of employment due to exports is larger than the average export ratio, then we can conclude that production for export tends to create more jobs than does production for domestic sales. This result is soundly confirmed by table 21. In manufacturing, exports accounted for 56.09 percent of total sales, but contributed 75.57 percent of total employment. The same finding holds true for all other industries except textiles; in some industries (apparel, wood, bamboo, and rattan products, and leather and leather products) both figures are very high and quite close.[4]

TABLE 20   MATERIALS-TO-SALES RATIOS OF FOREIGN FIRMS, BY LOCATION AND BY
             INDUSTRY, 1975
             (UNIT: PERCENT)

Industry	Foreign firms in EPZs	Foreign firms outside EPZs
Apparel	80.20	56.55
Plastic products	46.78	62.01
Metal products	44.57	54.38
Machinery	70.45	52.41
Electrical and electronics	78.07	53.98
Others	65.28	54.95
All industries	**75.60**	**54.57**

SOURCES: Same as for table 19.

TABLE 21   EXPORT RATIOS AND EMPLOYMENT DUE TO EXPORTS OF FOREIGN
             FIRMS, BY INDUSTRY, 1975
             (UNIT: PERCENT)

Industry	Employment due to exports (percent)	Average export ratios
Foods and beverages	46.87	20.77
Textiles	75.51	77.61
Apparel	97.38	96.84
Wood, bamboo, and rattan products	94.75	93.89
Paper and products	22.90	16.69
Leather and products	99.99	99.96
Plastic and rubber products	94.42	85.29
Chemicals	54.70	43.17
Nonmetallic products	32.60	8.58
Basic metals and products	62.92	50.13
Machinery	64.60	35.67
Electrical and electronics	77.08	63.56
Total	**75.57**	**56.09**

SOURCE: Investment Commission, MOEA, *Foreign Firm Survey,* 1975.
NOTE: Exports include indirect exports, which are defined as sales to exporting firms used in exports.

The same data permit us to calculate the number of employees per million dollars of either exports or domestic sales for foreign firms. The results, shown in table 22, indicate that the overall employment effect per million dollars' worth of exports is 120 persons, compared to 67 persons per million dollars of domestic sales. With the exception of textiles, for the same reasons given above, domestic sales in all industries always created less employment per dollar of sales than did exports.[5]

Against the foregoing derivation of the number of employees per million dollars of sales created, the objection may be raised that the same product may be sold abroad at lower prices than locally. Because of Taiwan's protection measures, this was indeed the case. The differences between domestic and export prices in Taiwan in 1973 varied from zero for highly export-oriented industries to 28.81 percent for the electrical and electronics industry (Schive 1979). When the data are

TABLE 22   NUMBER OF PEOPLE EMPLOYED BY FOREIGN FIRMS PER MILLION DOLLARS OF EXPORTS AND OF DOMESTIC SALES, BY INDUSTRY, 1975 (UNIT: PERSON)

Industry	Exports	Domestic sales	Domestic sales adjusted by nominal rates of protection
Foods and beverages	87.4	25.8	28.5
Textiles	77.1	86.6	100.3
Apparel	184.7	152.4	152.4
Wood, bamboo, and rattan products	185.8	158.8	158.8
Paper and products	112.9	76.0	76.0
Leather and products	264.1	42.0	42.0
Plastic and rubber products	198.0	68.0	80.6
Chemicals	57.8	36.5	39.1
Nonmetallic products	125.0	24.3	24.3
Basic metals and products	145.5	86.3	98.4
Machinery	120.0	36.5	37.6
Electrical and electronics	126.9	65.7	87.0
Total	**120.8**	**49.8**	**56.6**

SOURCES: Investment Commission, MOEA, *Foreign Firm Survey*, 1975; for the nominal rate of protection, see Schive et al. 1979.

NOTE: The nominal rate of protection is defined as the difference between the domestic and international prices as a percentage of the latter.

adjusted by this factor, the results do not change at all, as shown in table 22.

4.5 Summary

Foreign firms as a whole used more labor-intensive technology than national ones, not because foreign firms used less capital per unit of labor in individual industries, but because they were more heavily concentrated in labor-intensive industries than national firms were. On the basis of data for much more narrowly defined industries, however, foreign firms' various capital-labor ratios were not significantly different from those of their national counterparts. Nevertheless, the export sectors of foreign firms, at both the industry-level and more aggregated levels, clearly used less capital per unit of labor than did their domestic sales sectors. In line with this, foreign firms' exports created more employment per dollar of output than did their production for domestic sales. This conclusion does not change even after the data are adjusted for the price distortion due to protection.

4.6 Addendum: A Critical Review of the Work of Mason, Cohen, and Riedel

Mason (1973) compared fourteen pairs of national and foreign firms within the same industry in the Philippines and Mexico. Cohen (1973) conducted a similar case study of Korea that included four U.S., five Japanese, and ten Korean firms. Riedel's (1975) study was based on a survey of 445 Taiwanese export manufacturing firms. These authors compared foreign and national firms' factor intensities (proportions), factor productivities, import content, degrees of export orientation, and factor prices.

In his measurement of factor intensities, Mason took the ratio of wages paid to the flow of capital services as an index. The result did not show any significant difference between U.S.-owned and national firms. Riedel took the capital-labor ratio multiplied by the utilization rate. He found that foreign firms adopted a less capital-intensive technology than their domestic counterparts in the apparel, plastic-products, and metal-products industries. Cohen tried to use electricity consumption to measure the degree of mechanization, but he concluded that no significant differences existed between foreign and national firms.

In the measurement of factor productivities, Mason used total factor productivity, but reached no definite conclusion. Cohen used monthly data on output per worker to test whether a learning curve existed and discovered that, in general, one did. Riedel calculated output-labor ratios and reached results similar to the existing patterns of capital-labor ratios.

As for factor prices (referring mainly to wage rates), Mason found that, except for professional personnel, U.S. firms paid higher wage rates to executive, technical, skilled, semi-skilled, and unskilled personnel, and also hired more of them proportionately, except for skilled labor.

The only common finding that emerges from these studies is that foreign firms purchased more of their materials abroad than national ones. Mason found that the local content (in total cash outlays) was lower for U.S.-owned firms. Riedel found that import dependence (imported raw material and intermediate inputs as a percentage of total output value) was consistently higher for all foreign firms. Similarly, Cohen discovered that Korean firms tended to import less than their foreign counterparts.

There is a deficiency in Riedel's data. A careful examination of his primary data shows that a number of firms misreported equity values for their fixed assets. Since foreign firms located in EPZs usually have lower equity values, the misreported data would underestimate the actual fixed assets used by these firms, in comparison with national ones. In addition, several firms in EPZs rented buildings; thus the value of their fixed assets was also underestimated in this regard.

5

Singer's Investment in Taiwan

DFI is an effective channel for transferring technology that may have a great bearing upon the host country's economy.[1] This chapter, which focuses on a case study of one company, will delineate the transfer process and its possible effect and implications.

The Singer Company, an American multinational corporation famous for its sewing machines, set up a factory in Taiwan in 1963. Since then, Taiwan's sewing machine industry has grown quickly, outstripping Japan's as the world's largest producer in 1978. By 1981, Taiwan's sewing machine industry had reached a production level of 2,997,000 units, of which 98 percent were exported.

The success of Taiwan's sewing machine industry seems to be closely related to Singer's investment in it. Singer's production process, unlike that of most other foreign firms, which focused at that time mainly on assembly, has been rich in technological change and upgrading. Hence we will broaden our discussion to include technological diffusion and changes in industrial organization due to DFI. Finally, because cases like Singer's have not appeared in other industries, it is important that we make a detailed study of this interesting investment.

5.1 Determinants of Singer's Investment in Taiwan

In 1963, Singer set up its first fully-owned subsidiary in Taiwan, Singer (Taiwan) Ltd., to produce sewing machines. The initial capital outlay was $800,000, financed partly by the company's Swiss subsidiary. At the time of Singer's investment, Taiwan already had a group of small sewing machine producers, all family-owned. In 1962, these companies produced a total of 38,781 machines (MOEA 1970). Their production process was rather primitive. They did not use blueprints in manufacturing parts, and quality control was almost nonexistent. More serious, parts specifications were not uniform among producers. As a result of the noninterchangeability of parts, the assemblers sometimes had to use adjustment devices to adapt parts to different specifications. China Sewing Machine Company (later Lihtzer), then the largest assembler, once tried to institute standardization, but failed because of limited parts purchases and the lack of technological capability. A few critical parts like shuttle bodies and bobbin cases, which constitute the heart of the sewing machine, had to be imported.

When Singer first applied to set up its plant in Taiwan, it met strong opposition from domestic firms, which argued that, with 250 assemblers and parts suppliers in operation, Taiwan's industry already faced excess capacity and a saturated local market. Local producers feared they would be displaced by Singer, with its worldwide reputation, technological leadership, abundant capital, and installment marketing policy. Indigenous firms argued also that they already had sufficient technology, as evidenced by their ability to export. Thus, Singer's investment would not bring in anything new, nor would it improve the industry's technological standard.

Nevertheless, the government approved Singer's investment, for two reasons. First, Taiwan was still importing certain types of sewing machines in the early 1960s, and Singer's investment was expected to replace the imports and save foreign exchange. Second, as the technological leader in the sewing machine industry, Singer would improve the quality of local parts, and hence the technological level of the local industry, provided that the company purchased locally made parts. In approving Singer's application, the government imposed the following conditions:

1. By one year after its establishment, Taiwan Singer should be procuring 83 percent of its required parts from local suppli-

ers; providing them with standardized blueprints; and assigning experienced engineers to help establish work methods, prepare materials specifications, and inspect finished products.

2. Taiwan Singer would be obliged to supply local assemblers with its own locally made parts at prices no more than 15 percent above the prices of parts imported from Singer's other plants.

3. Taiwan Singer should export to the maximum degree possible.

As illustrated in table 23, Taiwan Singer fulfilled those conditions quite satisfactorily. In meeting the first requirement, Taiwan Singer's local content increased from zero in 1964 to 50 percent in 1965, 75 percent in 1966, and 80 percent in 1967. By 1969, Taiwan Singer was using only locally made parts, except needles for its straight-stitch model.

Second, Taiwan Singer began making shuttle bodies and bobbin cases in Taiwan. In 1970, the company sold these two parts to local assemblers at about 20 percent less than the price of the imported items. Later, other manufacturers were also able to produce these parts.

Third, Taiwan Singer's exports volume increased at a stable annual rate of 12 percent during the period 1964–1976. Before 1966, the company's exports accounted for more than 20 percent of Taiwan's total exports of sewing-machine units; since 1968, that share has dropped to about 10 percent. The company's export share in terms of value has continued to be twice its share in terms of units, however (see table 23). Thus Taiwan Singer's products sell abroad at about twice the price of other companies' products. Table 23 also reveals that, during its first two years, Taiwan Singer sold more sewing machines in the domestic market than abroad. That situation has changed since 1966. In 1975 and 1976, it exported 86 percent of its total output. Thus, Taiwan Singer has met its exporting obligation quite satisfactorily.

The change in the company's relative market shares of exports and local sales reveals the incentive for Taiwan Singer's venture. The fact that it sold more sewing machines locally than abroad during its first two years indicates that an attractive local market was perhaps the key factor in bringing Singer to Taiwan. While Singer had, in fact, had a local distributor long before its actual investment, a 33 percent tariff and import controls on certain models provided another incentive to invest.

TABLE 23   SALES AND EXPORTS OF TAIWAN SINGER AND LIHTZER

| | Taiwan Singer | | | Lihtzer |
| | Domestic sale | Export | Export | Export |
Year	volume (unit)	Volume (unit)	Value ($ million)	Volume (unit)
1964	4,987	1,250 (22.9)	0.03 (30.1)	— —
1965	11,149	6,170 (52.0)	0.19 (95.0)	— —
1966	8,493	17,094 (21.8)	0.67 (37.3)	— —
1967	12,023	26,119 (14.5)	0.86 (34.2)	— —
1968	9,683	40,377 (13.8)	1.80 (41.0)	— —
1969	8,662	41,588 (11.8)	1.48 (24.4)	140,000 (39.7)
1970	9,976	42,367 (11.1)	1.32 (23.0)	180,000 (47.0)
1971	10,302	68,689 (9.7)	2.29 (21.4)	240,000 (33.9)
1972	10,350	80,509 (8.4)	2.53 (15.6)	280,000 (29.1)
1973	13,200	93,522 (9.1)	3.40 (18.3)	360,000 (35.1)
1974	18,008	116,073 (9.8)	5.18 (17.4)	400,000 (35.7)
1975	18,245	104,584 (10.7)	5.38 (20.9)	320,000 (32.7)
1976	18,688	129,167 (7.4)	5.89 (13.7)	400,000 (23.0)

SOURCE: Singer Industries (Taiwan) Ltd.; Lihtzer Sewing Machine Co.
NOTE: Figures in parentheses are export shares. Lihtzer is the largest national firm which exports 100 percent of its products. Data for Lihtzer before 1968 are not available.

5.2 The Process of Technology Migration and Diffusion

When setting up its Taiwan plant, Singer sent experts in accounting, production management, and a host of other activities (see table 24). They helped organize the entire management and production systems and also trained the local employees.

Once its own plant was operational, Singer began to provide a wide range of technical assistance, free of charge, to other sewing-machine producers.

1. Taiwan Singer conducted numerous training classes and organized seminars for the parts suppliers. Training included the study of heat treatment, the inspection of finished products, the use of measurement instruments, and the introduction of new concepts and techniques of factory management.[2] In addition, under an existing program called "Cooperation Between Vocational High Schools and Local Industry," the

company has been training 150 bench workers and lathe turn-
ers every year since 1970.
2. Taiwan Singer provided standardized blueprints and the necessary measuring gauges to parts producers.
3. Taiwan Singer also provided a variety of other services to individual firms. These services included opening up Taiwan
Singer's tool room to parts suppliers to help them make tools
and fixtures; solving technical problems in casting; improving plating facilities and work methods; controlling the di-
mensions of arm shafts; providing foundry patterns made by
Singer's tool room; redesigning the punch presses and dies

TABLE 24   FOREIGN TECHNICAL VISITATION TO THE TAIWAN SINGER PLANT,
1964–1975 (UNIT: NUMBER OF PERSONS)

| | Supervising Singer Local Plant | | | | Advising Local Suppliers | | | |
Year	Production	Accounting	Quality control	Management	Production	Quality control	Other[a]	Total
1964	11	2	—	—	—	—	7	22
1965	1	2	—	—	1	—	6	10
1966	2	3	1	1	—	—	12	19
1967	2	1	2	3	4	2	8	17
1968	3	1	—	—	2	—	8	13
1969	10[b]	3	3	—	3	1	13	27
1970	10[b]	3	6[a]	—	3	1	25	45
1971	7	—	—	1	3	—	31	39
1972	3	—	—	1	—	—	20	23
1973	3	—	—	1	—	—	51	55
1974	8	—	—	—	3	1	22	31
1975	1	—	—	1	—	—	43	45

SOURCE: Singer Industries (Taiwan) Ltd.

NOTES:

a. A Singer technician might come to Taiwan to inspect Singer's plant and advise local parts
suppliers simultaneously. Those visitors whose functions were not specified were doing
periodic factory inspection, financial auditing or program reviews, or were trainees from
Singer's other plants.

b. During these years, specialists were sent from abroad to help establish the system of quality improvement in Taiwan Singer's plant and those of its suppliers. For the program of
quality control, see text.

used in producing bobbins; and setting up heat treatment equipment for making needles. (Liu 1968)

Most of this assistance was initially given by Taiwan Singer's local technicians. Later, various experts came from abroad expressly to help local parts suppliers (see table 24). The functions of those experts ranged from upgrading the quality of existing parts to developing new ones. Taiwan Singer itself ultimately became a technology exporter and began to train employees of other Singer subsidiaries. For example, the first group of staff and engineers in Singer's Indian and Indonesian plants was trained by Taiwan Singer.

Taiwan Singer had a vested interest in providing free technical assistance to its parts suppliers. Its primary motivation was to make sure that the quality of those parts was up to its own rigid specifications. In order to maintain the quality of the final product bearing the name "Singer," the company had to help its parts suppliers solve their technical problems. In order to further ensure the quality of parts, Taiwan Singer also instituted a program of strict self-inspection by the parts suppliers themselves and helped the suppliers set up quality control procedures. Even so, Taiwan Singer still inspected incoming parts.[3]

5.3 Effects of Technology Migration and Diffusion

The sewing machine industry in Taiwan has grown rapidly since Singer's investment. Stuck in a technological bottleneck, the industry was almost stagnant before 1964. Between 1964 and 1973, however, it grew at an average annual rate of 33.1 percent, and at 19.0 percent between 1974 and 1981. Production has fluctuated in the 1980s, and no clear trend can be detected.

As for exports, the industry could hardly have claimed to be in the foreign market before 1964. In the first ten-year period since then, however, sewing machine exports showed an average annual growth rate of 129.5 percent, and of 16.8 percent between 1974 and 1981. In fact, since 1971 the industry seems to have exported almost all of its output. Thus, exports have been the major source of growth for the industry (see table 25).

How can we account for this rapid increase in the production and export of sewing machines? The technological upgrading of the industry in the mid-1960s seems to have been responsible for this growth. Through its extensive technical assistance to parts suppliers, and the sale to assemblers of parts its own factory had developed, Taiwan

TABLE 25 PRODUCTION, SALES, IMPORTS, AND EXPORTS OF THE SEWING
MACHINE INDUSTRY IN TAIWAN, 1954–1985

Year	Production (1000 unit)	Imports Volume (1000 unit)	Imports Value ($ million)	Exports Volume (1000 unit)	Exports Value ($ million)
1954–1957	188	—	—	0.5	0.04
1959–1961	227	12	0.81	0.3	0.01
1962–1963	87	8	0.73	1.5	0.03
1964	91	8	0.53	5.5	0.18
1965	79	7	0.78	11.9	0.20
1966	125	11	0.88	78.6	1.99
1967	212	15	1.50	180.4	2.52
1968	361	27	2.33	293.1	4.40
1969	519	16	1.70	352.2	6.08
1970	629	27	3.10	383.3	5.75
1971	788	52	4.55	707.1	10.69
1972	916	41	4.43	962.3	16.19
1973	1,256	—	0.05	1,026.2	19.55
1974	1,222	2	0.42	1,186.3	31.32
1975	1,047	2	0.18	977.9	27.11
1976	1,379	14	0.60	1,733.7	43.06
1977	1,546	23	0.87	1,514.1	44.87
1978	2,008	2	0.20	1,979.0	69.42
1979	2,076	—	—	2,046.0	—
1980	2,193	—	—	2,189.0	—
1981	2,997	—	—	2,937.0	—
1982	2,444	—	—	2,429.0	—
1983	2,625	—	—	2,575.0	—
1984	2,903	—	—	2,849.0	—
1985	2,315	—	—	2,339.0	—

SOURCES: MOEA, *Monthly Bulletin of Industrial Production, The Republic of China*, various issues; Ministry of Finance, *The Trade of China (Taiwan District)*, various issues.

Singer led the way in this upgrading effort. As one of Taiwan Singer's competitors acknowledged:

> Taiwan Singer did a great job in standardizing specifications of parts as well as raising the quality of parts. Our company has tried to do the same thing but with a minimum of success. Taiwan Singer with

its international reputation very easily obtained the response and cooperation from parts manufacturers. Our company, along with Taiwan Singer's technical assistance to parts suppliers, provided them
the needed working capital. Our combined efforts promoted the
technological level of the whole industry dramatically.[4]

Taiwan Singer has a total of 140 parts suppliers, which represent
about 60 percent of the total number of parts producers, and all 140
have received technical assistance from Taiwan Singer in one form or
another. As one arm-shaft manager conceded, "Taiwan Singer has
rigid requirements on parts production. It offers higher prices for the
parts ordered and pays quickly. Taiwan Singer has helped us improve
parts quality and increase sales and profits" (Liu 1968).

Singer's presence in Taiwan has also greatly benefited other assemblers of sewing machines, who have been able to use parts developed by or with the assistance of Taiwan Singer in the assembly of
their own final products. This improvement in product quality has
made the vast export market available to indigenous producers, and
that fact has been instrumental in the rapid growth of the industry.

Despite the rapid growth of the sewing machine industry in Taiwan following Singer's entry into it, Taiwan Singer has not come to
dominate the industry. For example, although the company contributed 43.1 percent of the total value and 25.6 percent of the units of Taiwan's sewing machine exports in 1964–1966, the first three years of its
operation, its share decreased significantly in later years (see table 23).
Taiwan Singer's share of exports in terms of both value and units declined by 1969 to 24.4 and 11.8 percent, respectively. Between 1969
and 1976, the two measures remained at about 20 and 10 percent, respectively. With the drop in Taiwan Singer's share, other domestic
producers, including those in joint ventures with Japan, have begun
to account for a larger proportion of Taiwan's sewing machine exports.

Taiwan Singer was not in direct competition with other domestic
producers in the export market before the 1980s, but competition
among domestic firms was fierce. In February 1976, local exporters
reached a "gentlemen's agreement" to ease competitive pressure by
setting a floor F.O.B. export price of $16.00 per sewing-machine unit.
Because of its worldwide marketing network, Taiwan Singer could af-
ford to charge higher prices for its products, and did. In addition,
many domestic producers sold abroad through trading companies or
under different brand names; Lihtzer's products, for example, carried
the brand name "Brother." More importantly, Taiwan Singer and the
domestic exporters were selling in different foreign markets (see table
26). Taiwan Singer exported most of its products to developing coun-

tries, while domestic producers increasingly exported to developed countries.

Although Taiwan Singer has been selling an increasing portion of its output in the domestic market, again, it has not been competing directly with local producers. Because of the prestige of the name "Singer," the company has been selling its products at rates substantially higher than other Taiwanese producers. For example, in 1976 Taiwan Singer's straight-stitch model sold for about $100 in the domestic market; another firm's similar model sold at half that price.

While Taiwan Singer has not been in direct competition with domestic producers, it has nonetheless had a significant influence on them. The company's domestic counterparts took it as a model and tried to emulate or even outdo it in its own areas of strength. Their efforts had important positive effects on the industry's overall technical proficiency and led to the attainment of higher technical standards.

TABLE 26   EXPORT DESTINATIONS OF SEWING MACHINES MADE BY TAIWAN SINGER AND OTHER FIRMS, 1966, 1970, AND 1975 (UNIT: PERCENT)

Year	Taiwan Singer		Other firms	
	Country	Export share	Country	Export share
1966	Vietnam	73	Vietnam	50
	Philippines	12	Hong Kong	20
1970	Ghana	19	U.S.A.	18
	Nigeria	20	W. Germany	8
	Colombia	14	Singapore	7
	India	10	Chile	6
			Indonesia	42
1975	S. Africa	9	U.S.A.	26
	Australia	8	W. Germany	5
	Colombia	6	Saudi Arabia	4
	Indonesia	7	Egypt	5
	Malaysia	9	Iran	12
	Zaire	6	Nigeria	4
	Philippines	16		

SOURCE: Singer Industries (Taiwan) Ltd.; Ministry of Finance, *The Trade of China (Taiwan District)*.

Singer's investment in Taiwan induced other foreign producers to follow its example. Thus four major Japanese sewing machine producers set up Taiwan ventures in the 1970s.[5]

Did these Japanese subsidiaries contribute to the upgrading of the technological level of Taiwanese parts producers? The general feeling is that they came to Taiwan mainly to take advantage of the locally available high-quality, low-cost parts. They did not take steps like those of Taiwan Singer to help the local parts industry. Since the Japanese firms export all their output, their entry into Taiwan had to be motivated by Taiwan's strong competitiveness in the international market. The surge in Taiwan's sewing-machine industry, initiated by Singer and followed by Japanese firms, provides a perfect example of Vernon's celebrated product cycle hypothesis: the dominant position in the world sewing-machine industry has shifted from the U.S. to Japan to Taiwan as the technology has matured and DFI has taken place (Vernon 1966).

5.4 Limitations of Continuing Reliance on Foreign Firms for New Technology

There are limits to the extent to which foreign firms can be relied upon for a continuous infusion of new technology and improvement of the existing technology. Because of global considerations within their multinational setting, foreign firms often do not enjoy the same degree of freedom in decision making as their local competitors. They may, therefore, sometimes show inflexibility and suffer from internal delays when making important decisions. On the other hand, when a native firm tries to maximize its profit or sales, or to develop a new product, the firm itself is the decision maker. As a result, aggressive domestic firms may be able to get ahead of their foreign counterparts. This is what happened in Taiwan. For example, Lihtzer, Taiwan's largest producer of sewing machines, outpaced Taiwan Singer in at least two areas by the end of the 1970s: (1) Lihtzer implemented a new method of manufacturing aluminum arms, leaving Taiwan Singer far behind; and (2) that firm introduced the first free-arm sewing machine. (This design allows removal of part of the sewing surface, making sewing easier. At one point, Taiwan Singer considered acquiring the arms from Lihtzer.) In addition, Taiwan Singer produced only machines for home use, leaving the Taibo Machinery Co. free to introduce a high-speed sewing machine for industrial applications.

Further, introduction of new products or improvement of existing ones may not be compatible with a foreign firm's global strategy. For example, Singer used its Taiwan plant as a base for exporting to developing countries. Because of the nature of the market in these countries, Taiwan Singer was not required to bring out new models or to continually upgrade its old ones actively. By contrast, the domestic firms were selling everywhere, including in the United States and West Germany. To remain competitive in these markets, characterized by higher income levels and changing consumer preferences, they had to try constantly to improve the quality of their products and to bring out new models. Thus their freedom to search for potential new markets must have helped domestic firms achieve higher technical standards. Although Taiwan Singer has maintained its high quality, its products have changed little over the years. The company has lagged behind domestic firms in adopting new production techniques and in developing new models.

Nor can foreign firms be relied upon to diffuse special managerial skills, such as marketing expertise. Taiwan Singer demonstrated its superior marketing skills by selling its products at prices substantially higher than those of its domestic competitors. Given the segmented markets between Taiwan Singer and the rest of the producers, Singer was not at all concerned about the increasingly severe competition among local firms. In fact, the company's generosity in helping domestic firms may have been an example of its unparalleled marketing skills. Nevertheless, Taiwan Singer was not expected to, and in fact did not provide marketing assistance to, local producers.

5.5 Conclusion

Singer's investment in Taiwan to produce sewing machines is an instance of the successful transfer and diffusion of foreign technology in a developing country by a multinational enterprise. The establishment of Taiwan Singer in 1963 created significant potential backward linkages, and the new company helped this potentiality to materialize in a relatively short time by providing technical assistance to its suppliers. Taiwan Singer's extensive and wide-ranging technical assistance advanced the technological standard of Taiwan's entire sewing-machine industry and thus contributed to its growth.

Several factors contributed to Taiwan Singer's success. First, given the absolute technological superiority and unparalleled marketing skills of its parent company, Taiwan Singer was not afraid to offer technical assistance to the national firms. Second, Taiwan's sewing-machine assemblers and parts producers were receptive to new ideas and willing to change. They took advantage of the assistance Taiwan Singer offered and quickly upgraded their own technological standards. Finally, the technology provided by Singer involved little or no capital expenditures; in fact, 90 percent of Taiwan Singer's machines and tools were locally made. The technology was simply a matter of the proper operation of machines, quality control, metallurgy, and metal fabrication, and so forth. Because Taiwan Singer's technological superiority was not capital-intensive, its diffusion was not only easier but cheaper.

There are, however, disadvantages to relying excessively on foreign firms for continuing technical progress and the introduction of new products. For one thing, because they are owned by multinational corporations, foreign firms may not enjoy the freedom necessary to make important decisions about new products and processes. Further, the national interests of host countries may come into conflict with the global strategies of parent organizations. Thus direct foreign investment may be best suited to breaking through technological bottlenecks. In any event, it is essential to the continuous growth of the industries concerned that indigenous firms develop along with foreign companies, and that an open-door policy on DFI be maintained.

6

Linkage: Do Foreign Firms Buy Locally?

When a foreign firm is set up, its relationship, or linkage, to the local economy is threefold.[1] First, it hires a certain amount of local labor and uses a certain amount of local capital. The wages and interest a foreign firm pays in this connection are its contribution to the host economy, provided it does not crowd out local competition. Second, foreign firms may buy materials from local suppliers and/or sell their products to local processors. This is where the linkage theory comes in. The third type of linkage between foreign firms and their host economies is the acquisition and diffusion to local firms of DFI-imported technology. This "invisible" linkage was discussed in Chapter Five.

In extreme cases, however, the situation is different:

> With little economic contact with the local economy, foreign investment occupies an enclave, tightly bound to the home country, far away, but only loosely connected, except geographically, to the local scene. (Kindleberger 1968, p. 146)

When DFI in LDCs is restricted to foreign enclaves, and linkage to the host countries is limited to the use of local labor and capital, no further positive influence can be expected. This has been a common phenomenon in foreign-controlled extractive, export-oriented, and plantation operations in LDCs. In the case of Taiwan, with its poor endowment in natural resources, there have been no foreign extractive or plantation operations, but a large proportion of foreign businesses are export-oriented. What, then, are the characteristics of the foreign enclave phenomenon in Taiwan?

6.1   The Linkage Issue

In order to explore the physical linkages between the foreign and domestic sectors, we should examine Hirschman's concept of linkage effects (Hirschman 1958). Theoretically, firms in closed economies will acquire their intermediate inputs from each other; and, conversely, their outputs may be acquired by other firms for further processing. Thus a firm in a closed economy is bound to develop some links with others in one way or another. Consequently, an initial move to set up a pioneering industry or firm can induce a series of developments resulting in more investment and employment. This is what the linkage theory emphasizes.

To make the concept operational and identify the key sector (or industry) in this process, Hirschman divides linkage effects into two types, backward and forward, which are defined as follows:

> Backward linkage effects, i.e., every nonprimary activity, will induce attempts to supply through domestic production the inputs needed in that activity. . . forward linkage effects, i.e., every activity that does not by its nature cater exclusively to final demand, will induce attempts to utilize its output in some new activities. (Hirschman 1958, p. 100)

Of these two effects, backward linkages are usually given more weight. As regards new investment, for example, if the assurance of the market for output is more important to a potential foreign firm than the availability of local input, then backward linkages, by creating demand, will be more effective in stimulating further investment than will forward linkages, i.e., supplying local materials. This may be the case for most LDCs, because "economic development is constrained by a shortage of decision-making ability, particularly with respect to decision to invest" (Yotopoulos and Nugent 1973, p.157).

Elegant as the linkage theory is, however, it is severely limited by its assumption of a closed economy. The links between a newly established firm and the other firms in a closed economy may vanish in an open economy. The extreme case is a foreign enclave, in which neither backward nor forward linkage effects are working. The enclavistic aspect of DFI may, however, be directly in line with the host countries' comparative advantages; for example, even if all materials are imported, processing may still be done by the host country's abundant and inexpensive labor. Thus the fruitlessness of other types of linkage poses no problem in this case. In fact, during a certain phase, "every new development is initially an enclave and it takes time for all innovation to work through and be absorbed" (Meier 1970, p. 505). Enforcing linkage effects without regard to a country's comparative advantages will cause difficulties, as was the case with the import substitution–promotion policies of many LDCs.[2]

The paradox in the linkage argument when a static framework is assumed may be eliminated by giving the argument a dynamic setting. That is to say, linkages are, initially, merely potential effects, with no guarantee of realization. This is, in fact, what Hirschman meant by linkages, which he carefully defined as "attempts"; under no circumstances will these attempts bear fruit immediately. In the extreme case, linkages remain as potentials but are never realized (Weiskoff and Wolff 1977). However, the linkage theory asserts, as time passes, or as local conditions begin to favor the development of related industries induced by DFI, linkages do provide a strong incentive or stimulus to accelerate development.

A systematic approach to the linkage issue should focus on two points: (1) what are the potential impacts on others created by DFI?; and (2) to what extent do those potentialities materialize over time, and how do they do so? The second question deserves more attention than the first, especially in relation to backward linkages.

6.2 Linkages of DFI: The Static View

We can calculate an index of backward linkages by applying Rasmussen's formula to input-output tables (Rasmussen 1956, pp. 135-45). In essence, this index shows the share of an economy's total gross production which is absorbed by, or supplied to, a certain industry in response to its one-unit increase in final demand. For instance, building a car requires not only that the car be assembled, but that all the parts be produced or imported; these parts are direct inputs. Domestic production of these parts will, in turn, cause production of all the materials needed for those parts; these materials are indirect inputs. The process branches out from there, so that the production of a car ultimately requires a multiple of its actual production. The ratio of total gross production to final production can be used to measure the de-

TABLE 27   LINKAGE INDICES AND LEVELS OF DFI IN MAJOR INDUSTRIES, 1974

Industry	Backward-linkage index (percent)	Rank	Approved DFI ($ million)		Sales of foreign firms ($ million)		Market shares (percent)	
			Non-Chinese	total	Non-Chinese	total	Non-Chinese	total
Foods and beverages	.99	8	8	25	68	156	4.4	9.9
Textiles and apparel	1.17	2	32	83	238	373	6.6	10.3
Wood, bamboo, and rattan products	.81	11	3	8	16	27	5.2	8.7
Paper and products	1.03	6	4	8	7	10	1.5	2.0
Leather and products	1.07	5	3	9	6	18	3.0	10.4
Plastic and products	1.02	7	19	34	75	144	6.2	11.9
Chemicals	.91	9	143	156	202	292	21.3	30.7
Nonmetal products	.83	10	29	42	12	163	2.0	30.4
Primary metals	1.28	1	93	103	59	72	4.2	5.2
Machinery	1.11	4	100	107	103	107	7.9	8.1
Electrical and electronics	1.14	3	363	375	1,151	1,183	52.0	65.3
Rank correlation between linkage index and DFI			39.75	45.46	42.73	10.00	19.09	−21.82

SOURCES: Economic Planning Council, Executive Yuan, *Taiwan Input-Output Tables, Republic of China, 1974, 1975*; Investment Commission, MOEA, *A Study of Operations and Economic Effects of Foreign Enterprises in Taiwan, 1974*.

NOTE: For the formula used to calculate the backward-linkage index, see Rasmussen 1956. Data for approved DFI measure stock as of the end of 1974. All other relevant DFI data were measured in 1974.

pendency of a certain industry upon the whole economy, that is, its backward linkages.

Tables 27 and 28 present the *ex ante* backward-linkage index as calculated from Taiwan's input-output table for 1974 and 1984, including imported inputs in order to show the maximum potential impact. The forward-linkages index was not shown for two reasons: (1) as pointed out above, backward linkages are more effective in stimulating investment than forward linkages; and (2) forward linkages for capital goods cannot be measured properly by ordinary input-output tables, which exclude flows of capital goods.[3]

The industrial structure of DFI was measured using: (1) data for total approved DFI as of the end of 1974 and 1984; (2) sales; and (3) market shares of foreign firms in 1974 and 1984. Non-Chinese foreign firms were measured separately because they would be expected to create stronger linkages than "neighboring" investment by overseas Chinese.

Of the eleven manufacturing industries that existed in 1974, the primary-metals industry had the highest value for backward-linkage effects; textiles and apparel ranked second; and the bamboo-and rattan-products industry had the smallest value. The top four industries for non-Chinese investment were the electrical and electronics industry, chemicals, primary metals, and machinery. Non-Chinese investment dominated the electrical and electronics industry, with 52 percent of the market share, and controlled 21.3 percent of the chemicals-industry market.

The information presented in table 27 does not support any clear inference as to whether DFI has created strong backward linkages, by concentrating in those industries with greater demand for all the materials and parts needed, but some lesser conclusions can be drawn. First, although five out of the six coefficients ranking the backward-linkage index and various measures of DFI industrial composition are positive, none of them is statistically significant. Second, we find from data for approved DFI that four out of the five industries with heavy foreign investment (textiles, machinery, chemicals, primary metals, and the electrical and electronics industry) fill the top four places for backward linkages (the exception is the chemicals industry). Moreover, the backward-linkage index for all foreign firms, weighted by sales, is 1.09. Given these findings, it is probable that DFI provided moderately stronger backward linkages in the 1960s and early 1970s.[4]

The 1984 data presented in table 28 do not alter previous conclusions. The plastic and plastic products industry exerted the second-strongest backward-linkage influence on other industries. After ten years, the chemicals industry, formerly weak in its backward linkages

TABLE 28   LINKAGE INDICES AND LEVELS OF DFI IN MAJOR INDUSTRIES, 1984

Industry	Backward-linkage index	Rank	Approved DFI	
			Non-Chinese	Total
			(US$ million)	
Food and beverages	1.1141	7	84	121
Textiles and apparel	1.2275	4	35	95
Wood, bamboo, and rattan products	0.9747	10	6	23
Paper and products	1.1133	8	12	23
Leather and products	1.2474	2	4	7
Plastic and products	1.2385	3	102	122
Chemicals	1.0646	9	716	757
Nonmetal products	0.9638	11	53	329
Primary metals	1.3013	1	265	302
Machinery	1.1245	5	481	506
Electrical and electronics	1.1243	6	1,347	1,378
Rank correlation between linkage index and DFI			0.063636	−0.15455

Industry	Sales of Foreign Firms		Market Shares	
	Non-Chinese	Total	Non-Chinese	Total
	($ million)		(percent)	
Food and beverages	247	470	2.39	4.55
Textiles and apparel	871	1,303	7.40	11.07
Wood, bamboo, and rattan products	37	50	1.70	2.31
Paper and products	54	104	1.79	3.44
Leather and products	23	73	1.67	5.22
Plastic and products	434	675	6.15	8.01
Chemicals	1,491	2,202	10.59	15.64
Nonmetal products	248	534	9.67	20.76
Primary metals	364	477	3.25	4.26
Machinery	1,543	1,614	22.13	23.15
Electrical and electronics	4,916	5,065	56.70	58.42
Rank correlation between linkage index and DFI	0.10000	0.04546	−0.12727	−0.03636

SOURCES: Directorate-General of Budget, Accounting and Statistics, Executive Yuan, *Taiwan Input-Output Tables, 1984*; Investment Commission, MOEA, *Business Situation and Economic Impact of Overseas Chinese and Foreign Enterprises in Taiwan: A Survey Report, 1984*; Investment Commission, MOEA, *Statistics on Overseas Chinese and Foreign Investment, Technical Cooperation, Outward Investment, Outward Technical Cooperation, 1974 vs. 1986.*

(ranking ninth out of eleven), became the fifth-strongest industry in that regard. Another unanticipated change was the move of the electrical and electronics industry from third place in 1974 to its rank of sixth in 1984.

Second, none of the rank-correlation coefficients between backward-linkage indices and measures of DFI activity were significant, though all had positive values. The weighted average of the backward indices (by cumulated DFI) between 1974 and 1984 remained at 1.15. Thus, despite the changes in Taiwan's industrial structure in that decade, DFI was at best only moderately correlated with industries that have significant backward linkages.

6.3 Foreign Firms' Local Purchasing, 1972–1985

When the study of DFI linkage focuses on investors' intentions to realize backward linkages, the analysis of foreign firms' local purchasing over time presents a more promising approach to the issue. Table 29 shows that both the amount and the proportion of local contents (locally purchased materials over total materials) increased between 1972 and 1981, then stabilized. Over the ten years of the 1970s, the total amount of local purchasing increased 8.2 times; non-Chinese foreign firms performed even better, increasing their local purchasing 9.4 times. The change in local-content rates over time is a more significant

TABLE 29   FOREIGN FIRMS' LOCALLY PURCHASED MATERIALS: AMOUNTS AND RATIOS, 1972 AND 1985 (UNITS: $ MILLION, PERCENT)

| Year | Overseas Chinese | | Non-Chinese | | Total | |
	Amount	Ratio	Amount	Ratio	Amount	Ratio
1972	99	64.50	265	35.84	364	40.78
1975	177	53.57	580	45.63	757	47.28
1978	372	53.74	1,405	48.96	1,777	48.89
1981	615	52.98	2,763	53.52	3,378	53.42
1985	553	55.10	2,468	50.18	3,021	53.26

SOURCE: Investment Commission, MOEA, *An Analysis of Operations and Economic Effects of Foreign Enterprises in Taiwan,* various issues.
NOTE: Data for 1972 exclude foreign firms in EPZs.

finding. Foreign firms as a whole bought 40.78 percent of all their materials from local markets in 1972, but 53.42 percent in 1981 and 53.26 percent in 1985. It is noteworthy that the rise in local-content rates in the 1970s is attributable to non-Chinese foreign firms; overseas-Chinese firms maintained a stable local-content rate of around 54 percent between 1975 and 1985.

The data in table 29 have the defect that the 1972 data exclude firms in EPZs. Table 30 breaks down foreign firms by their locations. We find first that foreign firms in EPZs have constantly had lower local-content rates than those outside EPZs. On the other hand, the rise in local-content rates between 1975 and 1978 was greater for foreign firms in EPZs than for those outside them. Second, for firms outside EPZs, non-Chinese foreign firms showed a constantly rising trend for local-content rate, while overseas-Chinese firms had a slightly declining trend. Third, non-Chinese foreign firms had local-content rates constantly lower than those of overseas-Chinese firms; that distinction between the two groups vanished in EPZs, however.

All these findings lead to the conclusion that foreign firms in EPZs, and non-Chinese firms in general, performed more like enclaves than did foreign firms outside EPZs and overseas-Chinese firms. That situation improved quite satisfactorily over a short period of time, however.

TABLE 30   FOREIGN FIRMS' LOCALLY PURCHASED MATERIALS (AMOUNTS AND RATIOS), 1972–1978, BY LOCATION (UNITS: $ MILLION, PERCENT)

Year	Overseas Chinese		Non-Chinese		Total	
	Amount	Ratio	Amount	Ratio	Amount	Ratio
1972:						
Outside EPZs	99	64.50	265	35.84	364	40.78
1975:						
Inside EPZs	15	29.04	65	29.59	80	29.48
Outside EPZs	163	58.16	515	49.00	678	50.94
1978:						
Inside EPZs	27	36.43	162	35.30	189	35.46
Outside EPZs	345	55.83	1,243	51.56	1,588	52.43

SOURCE: Primary-data survey of Investment Commission, various years.

TABLE 31   FOREIGN FIRMS' LOCAL CONTENT RATE, 1972–1978, BY INDUSTRY
            (UNIT: PERCENT)

	1972	1975	1978
Textiles	37.73	31.47	40.72
Garments	68.32	59.19	59.97
Plastic and rubber	78.34	74.55	65.41
Chemicals	53.48	65.29	65.58
Basic metals	25.40	35.79	35.87
Machinery	60.92	57.17	50.88
Electrical and electronics	33.13	46.04	50.19
Foreign firms (total)	**40.78**	**50.94**	**52.43**

SOURCE: Same as for table 27.
NOTE: Data for 1975 and 1978 exclude foreign firms in EPZs.

Table 31 presents a breakdown by industry for non-EPZ foreign firms' local-content rates between 1972 and 1978. In general, the garment, plastic and plastic-products, and chemical industries had relatively high local-content rates, but in the first two industries that proportion declined over time. The basic metals and textiles industries had the lowest local-content rates, but the local-content ratio of the former increased by 10 percent between 1972 and 1975. The electrical and electronics industry, which began with a low local-content rate, quickly switched its procurement policy from imports to local supplies during the brief period observed.

6.4 Do Older Firms Buy More Local Products?

The dynamic approach to linkage points out that time is an important consideration in foreign firm's local purchasing: it takes time for them to understand the local materials markets and to find suppliers, unless, of course, their investors have been motivated by strong local-materials markets from the very beginning and have come specifically to take advantage of them. Even in that case, it may be argued that time still favors existing firms over newcomers. Is this hypothesis borne out by the facts?

Table 32 presents the local-content rates of foreign firms according to their years of establishment. Both the total for manufacturing and the data for the electrical and electronics industry show that foreign firms established during different time periods have had different local-content rates. Foreign manufacturing firms established before 1966 had a much higher local-content rate than the average, while firms established in 1967–1975 had lower-than-average rates. Firms established since the late 1970s have shown increasing local-content rates.

Roughly the same picture appears in the electrical and electronics industry, with two differences: (1) the average local-content rate is lower in that industry than for manufacturing as a whole; and (2) the foreign firms with the lowest local contents were set up between 1976 and 1977, two years later than the corresponding low for total manufacturing.

The above findings reveal more than we might have expected. They indicate unmistakably that foreign firms with at least fifteen-years experience bought more local products than did latecomers. Thus time does help foreign firms establish links with the domestic economy. More important, recently established firms have shown an increasing tendency to buy from the local markets. One explanation is that these firms moved to Taiwan specifically for the competitive local products. In fact, a survey of foreign firms in the early 1970s revealed

TABLE 32   LOCAL CONTENTS OF FOREIGN FIRMS BY YEAR OF ESTABLISHMENT
(UNIT: PERCENT)

Founded	Electrical and electronics	Total manufacturing
Pre-1961	52.91	59.18
1961–1966	51.65	61.75
1967–1971	38.06	50.50
1972–1973	39.49	46.65
1974–1975	40.85	38.46
1976–1977	22.84	46.71
1978–1979	50.78	49.56
1980–1982	33.07	42.58
Total	39.94	49.03

SOURCE: Primary data of foreign-firm survey by Investment Commission, 1982.

that local-materials markets influenced those firms' selections of locations (Koh 1973). A study of Taiwan's materials and capital markets indicates that Taiwanese manufacturers as a whole have relied less upon imported materials since the late 1970s—a phenomenon called secondary import substitution (Schive 1987 and forthcoming).

Thus foreign investment in Taiwan has had both kinds of linkage effects. Earlier DFI, once established, has created a potential market for materials, which have gradually come to be supplied by local producers. That growing local-materials industry has, in turn, attracted new foreign investors to use its products—forward linkage—as evidenced by the fact that 10–15 percent of the aggregate production that foreign firms sold to downstream producers ended up as exports (see table A-2).

The above findings raise a concern about table 30: If the founding dates of foreign firms influence the local contents of their products, then the survey results for different years will be affected by this "timing" factor. Table 33 shows that, after recently established firms have been eliminated from the sample, non-Chinese foreign firms still bought progressively more local products.

6.5   Other Factors Affecting Foreign Firms' Local Purchasing

Apart from factors such as location, investor status, and investment duration which clearly affect foreign firms' local purchasing, many other factors may play a role in this regard. As we have defined a foreign firm as a company with any amount of foreign capital participation, it should be pointed out that a firm wholly owned by foreign capital will behave differently than one in which foreign ownership is in the minority. The former is likely to leave most of its decision, including those on materials procurement, up to the parent company; minority-owned firms, however, do not have parent companies, but only foreign partners. Because of the greater familiarity of local partners in joint ventures and of minority-owned foreign firms with the local-materials markets, the local contents of foreign firms are assumed to vary negatively with increasing foreign ownership.

Because exports face more competition than products sold in the home market, the higher standards for the quality of their components may reduce local content. In terms of the policies regulating and/or encouraging local purchase, around ten products of the electrical and electronics and the machinery industries are subject to Tai-

TABLE 33   LOCAL CONTENTS OF FOREIGN FIRMS ESTABLISHED AT THE SAME TIME,
1972–1978
(UNIT: PERCENT)

Survey years	Overseas Chinese	Non-Chinese	Total
1972:	64.50	35.84	40.78
1975:			
Firms establ. before 1972	57.73	48.55	50.43
Firms establ. before 1975	58.16	49.00	50.94
1978:			
Firms establ. before 1972	54.81	52.04	52.41
Firms establ. before 1975	56.72	51.96	52.65

SOURCE: Same as for table 32.
NOTE: Excludes firms outside EPZs.

wan's local content regulations; that is, local production of these goods must meet certain local-content rates.[5]

These regulations exempt products for export, however. That is, all the materials and parts needed to produce an export can be imported without tariff. Therefore, the more of its products a firm exports, the lower its local-content rate will generally be.

Many materials and parts industries benefit from being large. These economies of scale, however, constrain development of indigenous parts industries; thus company size may help overcome the scale constraints of upstream industries. While it may also be argued that the large size of a downstream processor may make it difficult for its materials suppliers to meet its demand, these difficulties are only temporary in nature. Unless the quality of materials varies as demand increases, there presumably exists a positive relationship between local-content rate and company size.

When a final-goods industry creates backward linkages, those effects generally begin to materialize with the industry's major direct inputs (as with production of major parts for the car industry), and then with the materials needed for parts. This sequence of backward development is clearly observable in Taiwan and Korea (Schive, forthcoming). We would expect, accordingly, that a maker of final products would tend to have a higher local-content rate than a materials producer.

Table 34 presents the results of single variable–regression analysis of data from the 1975 and 1978 surveys of foreign firms in seven industries; these results confirm the above hypotheses to a large extent. For simplicity's sake, we have not presented each coefficient, but only its sign and level of statistical significance. These measures indicate that non-Chinese foreign firms with high export propensities and high foreign ownership that were located in EPZs and established after 1965 to produce parts or materials had a strong tendency to buy less locally. There are several exceptions, however. For example, statistically significant measures show that old textile mills also bought less locally. A detailed examination of the data reveals that several old cotton-weaving mills imported a large proportion of their cotton fiber because no local substitutes could be found. Scale factors were consistently significant for textiles, garments, and basic metals, but not for electrical and electronics products. One of the likely explanations is that large firms had diversified product lines, which militated against local purchasing. Another possible reason is that large firms, as measured by sales, shared some common features, such as majority ownership and EPZ bases, that do not favor local procurement.

With two years' data, we may include a dummy variable to separate the data for different years in order to test whether foreign firms bought more as time passed. The multiple-regression results in table 35 indicate, first, that the signs of the coefficients representing the time factor are positive, though insignificant. Second, all of the statistically significant explanatory variables have the expected signs. The results suggest that firms located in EPZs, with higher foreign ownership, more recently established firms, and intermediate-product producers tended to buy less in the local market. Another finding is the low R-2s for all industries, which implies that our hypothesis has to a large extent failed to explain the variation in foreign firms' local-content rates. A further implication is that some product-specific characteristics such as life-cycle and technology requirements may have significant effects on local-materials procurement.

6.6 Summary

Linkages are important potential impacts of DFI upon host economies. Because these potentialities are not necessarily realized, however, we must separate the potential (*ex ante*) and actual (*ex post*) results of these effects. Empirical data for Taiwan in the 1970s and early 1980s show that DFI may tend to concentrate in industries with

TABLE 34 SIMPLE REGRESSIONS ON DETERMINANTS OF FOREIGN FIRMS' LOCAL CONTENTS FOR VARIOUS INDUSTRIES

Industry	Year	No. of firms	X_1 Export ratio (%)	X_2 Foreign ownership (%)	X_3 Scale (sales, $)	X_4 Location in EPZs (dummy)	X_5 Year of establishment (dummy)	X_6 Final or intermediate products (dummy)	X_7 Overseas Chinese or non-Chinese DFI (dummy)
Textiles	1975	41	−	−	−**		−**		+
	1978	38	+	−	−*		−**		−
Garments	1975	53	−	−**	−**	−**	+		−
	1978	39	+	−	−	−**			+
Plastics and products	1975	57	−	−	−	−**	+	+	−
	1978	65	+	−	−	−**	−	+	+
Chemicals	1975	69	−	+	−	−	+	+	−*
	1978	83	−	−	+	−	+	+	−*
Basic metals	1975	76	−*	−*	−*	−*			−*
	1978	91	−	−*	−**		+		+
Machinery	1975	44	−*	−**	−	−**	+**	+	+
	1978	53	−**	−**	−	−**	+**	+**	+
Electrical and electronics	1975	153	−**	−**	+*	−**	+**	+**	−
	1978	178	−**	−*	+	−**	+**	+	−**

SOURCE: Same as for table 32.

NOTES: X_4 = 1 if located in EPZ; = 0 if elsewhere.
  X_5 = 1 if established before 1965; = 0 if established later.
  X_6 = 1 if final product; = 0 if otherwise (distinction cannot be made for textiles and garments).
  X_7 = 1 if overseas Chinese; = 0 if non-Chinese.

  * — significant at the 5% level.
  ** — significant at the 1% level.

TABLE 35   MULTIPLE REGRESSIONS ON DETERMINANTS OF FOREIGN FIRMS'
LOCAL CONTENTS FOR 1975 AND 1978

Year	Constant	Foreign ownership	Location in EPZs	Year of establishment	Final or intermediate products
1975	0.4101	−0.1502		0.1671	0.1267
	(6.96)**	(−2.15)**		(2.85)**	(2.41)**
1978	0.3837		−0.0790	0.1422	0.1160
	(12.66)**		(−1.67)*	(2.05)**	(2.07)**
1975 and 1978	0.4085	−0.1209		0.1361	0.1341
	(7.48)**	(−2.02)**		(2.77)**	(3.18)**

Year	1978 dummy	R^2	F
1975		0.128	8.43**
1978		0.60	4.79**
1975 and 1978	0.0341	0.105	8.44**
	(1.01)		

SOURCE: Same as for table 32.
NOTE: 1975 and 1978 sample covers only firms that appear in the surveys for both years. For meaning of asterisks, see table 34.

strong backward linkages. More significantly, DFI located in EPZs or controlled by non-Chinese investors had a clear tendency to import more and, hence, tended to form enclaves. However, this group of firms greatly improved its procurement policies over time. Thus, while discernible in the short run, the enclavistic phenomenon linked to DFI becomes insignificant in the long run, as Taiwan's experience shows.

In addition to the time factor, foreign-ownership structure, export propensity, status as a producer of either final or intermediate goods, status as a "neighboring" or "distant" investor, and the scale of operation all have a bearing on foreign firms' local-purchasing behavior.

7

Taiwan's Outward Investment: Native Multinationals

Taiwanese companies began to go abroad at a significant level only in the 1970s, about ten years after the surge of DFI into Taiwan.[1] By 1984, the total outward investment remitted was $117 million—54 percent of the approved amount, or 7.6 percent of the arrived DFI up to that time. Outward investment as measured by official data, however, is seriously underestimated. For example, one source shows that Taiwan's DFI in Thailand amounted to $52 million in 1970-1975 alone (Edwards 1977, p. 42); the official figure is $2.2 million. Vernon's study indicates that there were a total of 178 Taiwanese MNCs in Thailand by 1978; official statistics show 23 investment projects approved and 14 having begun operations, with five surviving as of 1981 (Vernon 1977, p. 27). Under these circumstances, the quality, not the quantity, of data should be emphasized. Case studies and questionnaires are useful for this purpose.

After a brief discussion on the trend of Taiwan's outward investment, this chapter will examine the motives and the industrial organization of Taiwan's MNCs. Because Taiwan's foreign ventures have been concentrated largely in ASEAN countries (Singapore, Thailand, Malaysia, the Philippines, and Indonesia), their competitiveness and the technology characteristics of that region will be explored. A company case study will be presented to illuminate the general findings reached. Finally, the prospects for Taiwan's outward investment will be examined.

7.1 The Trend of Taiwan's Outward Investment

Officially, the first Taiwanese outward investment was made in 1959 when a local firm invested $100,000 worth of machinery in a Malaysian cement plant. After a lull of two years, a jute-bag manufacturer restarted Taiwan's capital outflow in 1962 by setting up a plant in Thailand. Throughout the 1960s, Taiwan's direct foreign investment hovered around $800,000 annually. Outward investment has been increasing at an annual rate of 23.78 percent since the early 1970s, however.

By the end of 1981, the government had approved a total of 163 investment applications; of these firms, 48 (29 percent) were then no longer in existence.[2]

Of these defunct ventures, 35 had actually gone into operation, but the investors had withdrawn due to the failure of the business, or the outcome of the Vietnam war. Formosa Plastics, the largest manufacturing concern among the 54 local companies with at least one subsidiary by the end of 1981, had applied for twelve foreign ventures, but only four of these were in operation at that time. Since then, a series of investments in the U.S. petrochemicals industry has been initiated, with a total capital commitment of $24 million. Taiwan's second-largest manufacturing MNC, Tatung, had eight projects approved and in operation by 1981. Since then, Tatung has added an Irish TV plant to its worldwide network. Pacific Wire and Cable Co., the third largest Taiwanese MNC in manufacturing, had five projects approved, but dropped one of them by 1981. This company began a new trend in Taiwan's outward investment by setting up a high-tech joint venture, Mosel, in the Silicon Valley (Schive and Hsueh 1987). In the trade industry, a semigovernmental trading company set up a worldwide network of twelve overseas subsidiaries.

In general, the United States received the lion's share, 40.7 percent, of Taiwan's outward investment by 1981, with five ASEAN countries accounting for another 32.6 percent. The remaining investment is distributed mainly in Latin America and Africa (see table 36). As regards the industrial structure of Taiwan's outward investment, 24.1 percent of the remitted capital went to the electrical and electronics industry, 53.7 percent of which was located in the United States. The chemical, trade, nonmetallic-products and plastic-products industries attracted between 12 and 16 percent of the total outward DFI (see table 37).

TABLE 36   APPROVED AND REMITTED OUTWARD INVESTMENT, 1959–1985, BY COUNTRY
(UNITS: $ MILLION, CASES)

Outward investment	Total	ASEAN countries						U.S.	Others
		Thailand	Malaysia	Singapore	Philippines	Indonesia	Total		
Approved:									
by 1981:									
Amount	112.1	4.9	3.1	7.8	9.8	10.9	36.5	45.6	29.9
Cases	163.0	23.0	18.0	20.0	8.0	10.0	79.0	28.0	56.0
by 1985:									
Amount	214.2	9.5	7.3	9.3	10.1	25.8	62.0	117.2	35.8
	219.0	26.0	19.0	23.0	9.0	12.0	89.0	60.0	70.0
Remitted:									
Amount	59.9	2.6	2.9	7.5	0.7	5.4	19.1	27.1	13.7
Cases	114.0	14.0	12.0	16.0	6.0	4.0	52.0	26.0	39.0

SOURCES: Schive 1982, p. 10; Investment Commission, MOEA, *Statistics on Overseas Chinese and Foreign Investment, Technical Cooperation, Outward Investment, Outward Technical Cooperation, ROC.*

NOTE: Post-1875 outward investment data include significant amounts of portfolio investment, which cannot be distinguished from direct investment.

TABLE 37 TAIWAN'S OUTWARD INVESTMENT REMITTED, 1959–1981, BY INDUSTRY AND COUNTRY (UNITS: $1,000, PERCENT)

Industry	Total	ASEAN countries						U.S.	Others
		Thailand	Malaysia	Singapore	Philippines	Indonesia	Total		
Food and beverages	933 (1.8)	63	—	—	—	—	63	25	12
Textiles	337 (0.7)	—	28	—	—	—	28	65	7
Garments and footwear	256 (0.5)	—	—	77	23	—	100	—	—
Wood, bamboo, and rattan products	2,041 (4.0)	5	87	3	—	—	95	—	5
Paper	1,960 (3.8)	—	—	—	—	100	100	—	—
Plastic products	6,566 (12.8)	—	—	11	1	4	16	84	—
Chemicals	8,343 (16.3)	—	—	5	—	—	5	95	—
Nonmetal products	6,977 (13.6)	—	—	20	—	—	20	7	73
Primary metals and products	1,013 (2.0)	—	—	52	—	29	81	19	—
Machinery	50 (0.0)	—	—	—	—	—	—	100	—
Electrical and electronics	12,339 (24.1)	2	1	16	1	—	20	53	27
Trade	7,383 (14.4)	—	—	3	1	—	4	81	15
Construction, finance, services, and others	3,085 (6.0)	—	—	—	—	—	—	2	98
TOTAL	**51,256**								

SOURCE: Schive 1982.

7.2 Motives for Outward Investment

Taiwan's investors went abroad for four primary reasons: (1) to secure supplies of raw materials; (2) to pursue profits by supplying host-country markets; (3) to facilitate exports; and (4) to have access to technology in its country of origin. The first category of investors includes plywood producers, a fishing company, and a pineapple canner. Thailand, Malaysia, Indonesia, and Costa Rica are the host countries to these ventures.

Formosa Plastics initiated a $24 million series of investments in the United States with its acquisition in 1983 of a vinylchloride monomer (VCM) plant. Part of the VCM produced was shipped back home. This investment, therefore, can be considered as taking advantage of low materials costs (that is, the low prices of ethylene and energy).

Firms in the food and beverage, textile, plastic and plastic-products, and nonmetallic-materials industries were motivated to invest overseas by the desire to supply the domestic markets of the host countries. The major investors in the food and beverage industry are monosodium glutamate (MSG) producers, while the leaders in the textile industry process synthetic fibers. Several investors in the plastics industry are also interested in foreign investors. One plastic-products processor has three foreign subsidiaries. Most of the firms in the nonmetallic-materials industry are cement manufacturers.

To make this type of investment, a parent firm must have sufficient experience and technology to compete with local firms and other MNC subsidiaries. The Taiwanese investors in these four industries share the common characteristic of a long period of development and experience in their areas. For example, the MSG and cement industries were established by the 1950s, and the PVC and PE plastics industries were well developed by the late 1950s and late 1960s, respectively. The synthetic-fiber industry underwent rapid growth in the late 1960s, until it was supplying up to 90 percent of local demand (Schive 1978, p. 126). Thus, investors in the four industries were equipped with the necessary technology and marketing experience before they ventured into the relatively risky foreign market.

The third type of outward investment is aimed at facilitating exports of Taiwanese goods. DFI in the electrical and electronics and the trade industries can be classified in this category. As table 37 indicates, the United States attracted 53 percent of Taiwan's outward investment in the electrical and electronics industry, and 81 percent in trading. With the U.S. market absorbing around 40 percent of Taiwan's total exports in 1970, it was seen that the imposition of import quotas on Taiwanese goods would impede that country's trade. As a result, trading partners established subsidiaries to bring the United States into semi-finished products, which are not as tightly restricted, so that the restriction of Taiwan's exports by trade barriers would be reduced. Taiwan's three leading electrical and electronics producers all have ventures in the United States, and other large exporting manufacturers are eager to set up trading offices in their major export markets. For instance, Lihtzer, Taiwan's largest sewing machine maker (see Chapter Five), organized a trading company in the United States in the mid-1970s.

Another way to penetrate the fenced markets of major trading partners, particularly those with quota systems, is "quota hopping": Taiwanese exporting companies may set up offshore production in other countries to bypass quota restrictions. This has been the case for Taiwan's footwear industry in Latin America and, more recently, the Caribbean, and for textile ventures established in Singapore and in some French colonies, which are aimed at the EEC market. This type of export-promoting investment relies upon materials from the parent company or from Taiwan.

The final type of motivation to become a MNC is often seen in the recently developed high-tech industries. In 1979, a private firm, United Microelectronics Co. (UMC), was organized to commercialize several innovations developed in Taiwan's government-funded research institute, the Industrial Technology and Research Institution (ITRI). To ensure the continuous inflow of advanced technology, UMC set up a subsidiary, Unicorn, in the Silicon Valley, and maintained close relations with three other R&D companies: Mosel, Qusel, and Vitelic, controlled by overseas Chinese in order to monitor new technology and to boost its marketing skills. Each of these three companies operates both in Taiwan's science-based industrial park and in Silicon Valley, and each uses domestic capital. All of these companies have successfully turned out a great number of patents for the design and manufacturing of very-large-scale integrated circuits (VLSIs) (Schive, forthcoming). This unusual type of outward investment can be explained only by the desire to access the U.S. technology market.

7.3 Industrial Organization of Taiwan's Multinationals

The necessary data are available to test several hypotheses relating to the outward investment of Taiwan's MNCs. Hymer and others have formulated a theory about the industrial organization of an outward-looking industry which asserts that a firm's specific advantages and the structure of the industry in which it operates have a great influence on its characteristics as a MNC (Hymer 1966; Kindleberger 1969; Caves 1971 and 1974). When a firm owns intangible assets such as knowledge, which is difficult to patent effectively but relatively easy to move from one national market to another, it will prefer to exploit them through DFI, rather than through licensing or direct exports. When the firm is operating in an oligopolistic environment, with a limited market and keen competition, its desire to go multinational will be further intensified. The relatively large fixed information cost required before a large firm is ready to develop such assets internationally provides still more incentive to expand abroad.

The industrial-organization approach offers several testable premises: First, MNCs from developing economies will be large in size, although not necessarily large by international standards. Second, outward investment is an important means not only of gaining competitiveness in foreign markets, but also of growing when domestic markets become increasingly crowded. Third, the low cost of labor and materials will not be a major factor, even for DFI in LDCs.[3]

Taiwan's outward-looking firms are, in fact, large relative to the other firms in their specific industries, as is shown in table 38. With the exception of firms in the timber and bamboo products, metals, and construction industries, the largest companies in all the industries listed became multinationals sooner or later. In the metals industry, a nut maker and a welding rod manufacturer were the largest companies in their specific areas. Moreover, all but five Taiwanese MNCs were among the top 500 companies in Taiwan when they went multinational. Many large companies not engaged in foreign ventures were either subsidiaries of foreign companies themselves, or they were public enterprises.

Table 38's ranking of Taiwanese MNCs (TMNCs) may underestimate their financial strength, because many TMNCs belong to large conglomerates, many of which compare in size with the top 1000 U.S. enterprises, as is shown by the 1979 data in table 39. Its 1979 sales of $781 million put Taiwan's largest conglomerate, the Formosa Plastic group, on a par with America's 290th-largest company at that time. The ten Taiwanese conglomerates listed in table 39 controlled a total of 34 percent of Taiwan's outward investment, as counted by subsidiaries, or 60 percent, as counted by the amount of investment. Both findings thus extend Hymer's hypothesis that DFI from developing economies tends to be made by the firms dominant within their domestic industries.

TABLE 38   RELATIVE SIZE OF TAIWANESE MULTINATIONAL CORPORATIONS,
BY INDUSTRY

Industry	Rank of firm in industry (by sales)	Rank of firm among Taiwan's top 500 firms (by sales)
Food and beverages	1,2,8,x,x[a]	11,19,63,101,125
Fiber	1	5
Textiles	1,3,7,x,x,x,x	6,54,170,366,453,483,y[b]
Textile printing and dyeing	1	50
Lumber and bamboo products	2,7	75,161
Plastic products	1,4,6	1,87,129
Chemicals	1,2,5,10	2,18,65,142
Cement	1,2,8	7,16,179
Glass	1	66
Metals	6,9,10,x,x	196,244,261,308,y
Machinery and equipment[c]	1,x	97,130
Cable and wire	1,2	23,24
Electrical and electronics	1,3,5,x,x	4,9,17,143,y
Construction	12,x	430,y
Trade	1,69	57,731
Retail and service	1,x	50,y

SOURCES: China Credit Investigation Co., *Top 500 Firms in Taiwan,* 1980; primary data from Schive 1982.
NOTES:
a. x = not among top ten firms in the industry.
b. y = not among Taiwan's top 500 firms.
c. Excluding transportation equipment.

7.4 Competition and Technology Transfer: Taiwan's Multinational Corporations in ASEAN Countries

Taiwanese firms in ASEAN countries face competition both from indigenous firms and from the multinationals of other countries. Intuitively, these firms would seem to be at a disadvantage when competing with DC multinationals, which possess not only more advanced technology, but also superior managerial and marketing skills and more favorable treatment in the international capital market.

TABLE 39   SIZE OF TAIWAN'S OUTWARD-LOOKING CONGLOMERATES

Industrial group	Sales ($ million, 1979)	Domestic rank	Equiv. rank of U.S. co.	Outward investment ($ million)	No. of Cases Approved	No. of Cases Existing
Plastics (A)	781	1	290	30.5	12	4
Textiles (A)	339	2	514	4.5	3	3
Textiles (B)	329	3	522	0.2	3	1
Electrical and electronics (A)	260	6	596	2.7	7	7
Textiles (C)	208	7	681	1.0	1	1
Wire and cable	191	1	707	1.6	5	4
Cement	191	8	826	4.7	2	1
Electrical and electronics (B)	166	10	763	1.5	1	1
Pulp and paper	150	11	826	0.6	1	1
Food and beverages	124	12	913	0.3	1	1

SOURCE: Same as for table 38.

If these assumptions are true, then what advantages do LDC multinationals have?

According to Chen (1983), Hong Kong firms have the following advantages when competing with DC multinationals in LDC host economies: (1) lower managerial costs; (2) better understanding of the host country; (3) more appropriate technology; and (4) better connections with local and world-market distribution channels (Chen 1983, p. 194). Tables 40 and 41 present TMNCs' motives for investing in ASEAN countries, and their competitive edge over MNCs from developed countries, respectively.

The first, second, and fourth most important reasons for investing in ASEAN countries related to the market factor. Investors were motivated largely by the need to create a new market or to use the host country as a base for exporting to a third country. A third motive was that protectionism in the host countries created pressure for original suppliers to maintain factories there. Taiwanese firms must be encouraged to go multinational by finding buyers for their used or depreciated machinery (see also Chapter Two on the capital composition of DFI in Taiwan). Surprisingly, Taiwan's MNCs rank considerations of the costs of labor and materials very low. That finding, however, is in line with Hymer's industrial-organization approach to DFI, which de-emphasizes cost factors.

The main competitive advantages TMNCs had over their DC rivals are in marketing factors: products better suited to host markets;

TABLE 40   MOTIVES FOR TAIWANESE INVESTMENT IN ASEAN COUNTRIES

Motive	Weighted Rating
Opening a new market	0.09
Promoting exports to a third country	0.81
Exporting machinery	0.78
Host-country market threatening protectionism	0.72
Improving image in home market	0.55
Competition from already-internationalized firms from home country	0.51
Access to cheap raw materials	0.43
Access to cheap labor	0.26
Diversification of business risks	0.11

SOURCE: Schive 1982.

NOTE: The questionnaire allowed three rankings: high (2 points); medium (1 point); and low (0 points). Weighted average figures are simple averages of these points.

TABLE 41   COMPETITIVE ADVANTAGES OF TAIWANESE MNCs IN RELATION TO DC
MNCs IN HOST COUNTRIES

Advantage	Weighted Rating
Product better suited to host market	1.15
Lower price of product	1.06
Better marketing channels	0.94
Equipment easier to operate	0.70
Lower operating costs	0.70
More appropriate management style	0.67
Lower salary for managers from parent firm	0.15

SOURCE: Same as for table 40.
NOTE: See note to table 40.

lower prices; and better marketing channels. This is exactly what Lall asserted as the "marketing advantages" of MNCs from LDC (Lall 1982, p. 37). Factors linked to operation and management style, which were considered of moderate importance, favor the greater familiarity with their host countries and the more appropriate technology of MNCs from LDCs. As has frequently been pointed out, these factors are, in fact, the weakest point of MNCs from DCs (Lall 1978, p. 238; Wells 1983, p. 22).

If the large-scale production techniques that MNCs from DCs always employ in their own countries mean the full utilization of economies of scale, then their adaptation to the smaller markets of host countries destroys this advantage and increases production costs. Furthermore, highly capital-intensive and automated production techniques may not be employed effectively in many host countries because local labor markets cannot furnish either the advanced technology or the skilled labor required. Thus when DC multinationals use the same technology in their overseas operations as they use at home, the result is often lower productivity, in terms of both labor and capital (Marsden 1970, p. 478). In this environment, it has been argued, smaller-scale, more labor-intensive technology ("intermediate technology") is more appropriate (Schumacher 1973). In other words, what the host country needs is technology that can be easily operated, and that costs less, even though it is not necessarily the most advanced.

Assuming that the value of equipment per worker (the capital-labor ratio) represents the degree of technological sophistication and the scale of operation, the data in table 42 support the "appropriate technology" argument. These figures indicate that fourteen (63.6 percent) of Taiwan's 24 subsidiaries in ASEAN countries applied a technology similar to that used by their local counterparts, while six companies (27.3 percent) used more capital per worker than local companies did. Compared to their home plants in Taiwan, however, only three subsidiaries (13.6 percent) had a higher capital-labor ratio. Thus, half of the six Taiwanese subsidiaries with higher capital-labor ratios than their local counterparts had to use a more labor-intensive technology than they would have in Taiwan.

Thus, Taiwan's investors in ASEAN countries tended to use technology that was either similar to, or more labor-intensive than, what they used at home. In both cases, the technology transferred is smaller in scale and easier to operate than the technology of DCs.

On a micro basis, Rhee and Westphal have found that the small-scale production techniques of these firms incorporate genuine innovations in machinery designed and manufactured in Taiwan (Rhee and Westphal 1978, p. 10). A Taiwanese synthetic-fiber maker's attempted investment in Indonesia provides a good example. In 1979 this company planned a joint venture with local businessmen in Indonesia, establishing a plant to manufacture polyester fiber. The equipment, actually a complete polyester-fiber plant valued at US$26 million, was exported from Taiwan. The interesting point here is that the technology employed had originally been imported from a DC, but through innovations, the Taiwanese firm had been able to manufacture the equipment at one of its affiliated workshops and at a lower

TABLE 42   FACTOR INTENSITY OF TAIWANESE SUBSIDIARIES IN ASEAN
COUNTRIES
(UNITS: NO. OF FIRMS AND PERCENT)

Taiwanese Subsidiaries	Home Plants	Local Firms
More labor-intensive	9 (40.9)	2 (9.1)
Similar	10 (45.5)	14 (63.6)
More capital-intensive	3 (13.6)	6 (27.3)

SOURCE: Same as for table 38.

cost. Obviously, many modifications were made, and local machinery and parts were used extensively (Ting and Schive 1981, pp. 112-13). This company may be a typical example of Taiwan's investment in ASEAN countries.

In sum, the main competitive advantages of these MNCs are their smaller-scale production techniques and their superior marketing and technological skills, which allow them to introduce and develop products welcome in the host markets. Because the technology brought in by Taiwanese MNCs is not as capital-intensive as that offered by MNCs from DCs, it is better suited to the basic conditions and comparative advantages of the host countries.

7.5 Tatung, Taiwan's Leading Multinational Corporation

The Tatung Company, a leading electrical and electronics manufacturer in Taiwan, is a multidivisional company with a large number of product lines ranging from household appliances, telecommunications equipment, electronics products and computers, to heavy electrical equipment and instruments, steel, machinery, and chemicals. In 1985, the company's gross sales amounted to US$640 million. Founded in 1918, it has steadily progressed to become a major industrial corporation in Taiwan and, through later foreign investments, to achieve the status of a technologically competent multinational firm.

In the early 1970s, Tatung began to establish a network of manufacturing subsidiaries in Japan, Singapore, Hong Kong, the United States, and Ireland, in addition to a global network of sales and purchasing offices in Europe, the Middle East, and Africa. By 1977, its overseas investments totaled about US$5 million. Tatung's entry into international business followed the classic pattern of development. Its success with exports led to technical cooperation and licensing of technical know-how and, subsequently, to direct investment. Its subsidiaries in Japan, Singapore, the United States, and Ireland primarily manufacture and assemble the same products, such as household appliances and electronic goods, with which it first attained domestic success.

Besides its manufacturing subsidiaries and its network of sales offices to service export markets, Tatung has also entered into technical-cooperation agreements and joint ventures with local manufacturers in several LCDs. These cases include technical assistance agreements and joint-equity ventures in electrical household appliances in Indonesia and Malaysia. A summary of Tatung's diverse international business ventures is presented in table 43.

A combination of factors seems to have spurred Tatung's multinationalization. The company's success in its domestic market appears to have provided the initial thrust, both by conferring upon it the ability to invest abroad and by engendering a need for it to internationalize in order to maintain an image of leadership and prestige among its competitors. A closely parallel reason was the reinforcement of its brand name in the international markets to which it had already been

TABLE 43   TATUNG'S OVERSEAS INVESTMENT, TECHNICAL COOPERATION, AND SALES SERVICING, 1984

Country	Investment[a] (US$1,000)	Form of business[b]	Products
Japan	102.8	WOS, SST	TVs, washing-machine, cooker, refrigerator reassembly
United States	1,353.0	WOS, SST	Color TV, electric fan mfg.
Hong Kong	108.3	WOS, SST	Color TV mfg.
Singapore	1,143.5	WOS, SST	TV–picture tube mfg., TV assembly
Indonesia	Technical fees	TA, EJV	TVs, transistors, stereos, transformers
Thailand	Technical fees	TA, EJV	TVs, refrigerators
Philippines	100.0	TA, EJV	Washing machines, rice cookers, electric fans, meters
West Germany	—	SST	Electrical household products, TVs, audio equipment
Korea	—	SST	Electrical household products, TVs, audio equipment
Ireland	—	WOS	Color TVs

SOURCE: Ting and Schive, 1981.
NOTES:
a. Investment includes plant, machinery and equipment, working capital, and land.
b. WOS = wholly-owned manufacturing subsidiary; TA = technical assistance; EJV = equity joint venture; SST = sales servicing, import/export, and retailing.

exporting. The immediate motive of circumventing the tariffs and quota restrictions of EEC and high-tariff LDC markets may also have contributed to Tatung's internationalizing its production. As European protectionism against Asian electronics exports went up, many Asian firms moved their plants to excess-quota countries in order to maintain their European sales from those locations. For instance, Tatung's television plant in Singapore was established both to circumvent the EEC quota and to supply completely knocked-down units to high-tariff countries in the region. Tatung's recent move into Ireland was motivated solely by the same goal.

As would be expected of a multinational corporation from a newly industrializing country (NIC) in the Asia-Pacific region, Tatung takes an ethnocentric approach to managing its subsidiaries. Most planning and control decisions are centralized in the Taipei headquarters, and only the necessary day-to-day operational decisions are made in the various subsidiaries. The company's personnel policies are also characterized by an ethnocentric orientation, and virtually all management and technical personnel of its foreign subsidiaries are Taiwanese nationals. This is due to the firm's being both culturally predisposed and economically motivated to use managers and technicians from Taiwan. The costs of maintaining its overseas personnel are much lower than are those of the advanced countries' multinationals. In addition, the nature of Tatung's investments in less-capital-intensive, smaller-scale, and general-purpose technology for its subsidiaries requires a great number of skilled personnel capable of improvisation to compensate for the lack of the specialized production equipment usually found in capital-intensive technology. Thus even operating-level technicians in the subsidiaries are home-country nationals.

Tatung is less sophisticated in its marketing, and more production- and process-oriented than MNCs from the developed countries. Compared with many local firms, however, it has demonstrated a high degree of marketing orientation. It has, for instance, cultivated its international reputation through the use of a well-designed brand name and logo. Brand recognition and awareness are relatively high in several of the LDCs of Southeast Asia and Europe, where many of Tatung's household and electronic products sell competitively against other well-known foreign brands.

Although it features no original R&D or new product innovation, Tatung nevertheless pursues a relatively sophisticated product-modification strategy. In the field of consumer electronics, for example, the company's product strategy involves the "scaling up" and "scaling down" of product features and designs to meet the specific needs of different levels of consumer sophistication. Its department for adaptive R&D and product modification, the largest in Taiwan, had a $17.6 million budget in 1984.

As an NIC, Taiwan has acquired the capability to provide production technology to LDCs and to other NICs. Technology transfers by firms from newly industrializing nations usually gravitate toward the intermediate-technology industries of the recipient economies, and are usually more efficient providers of products and processes at the lower and intermediate ranges of the technology spectrum. A NIC firm's technological compatibility with the recipient stems from the similarities in their general economic development and technology. It is often more efficient to transmit technology to LDCs via the more advanced developing countries rather than directly from advanced countries because of the wide technological gap between them. Thus, Taiwan has been perceived as a bridge in the technology-transfer process. It receives, absorbs, and adapts advanced technology from the industrialized countries; then transmits it in a scaled-down and modified form to other developing nations.

NIC multinationals are more efficient suppliers of modified or intermediate technology because of their cost economies in the transfer process. Their investments are usually small-scale and less capital-intensive than those of their advanced-country counterparts. They also incur lower overheads in terms of less-expensive overseas personnel and facilities (Wells 1978). On the side of consumption technology, multinationals from NICs may have superior market knowledge, especially as regards standardized, mature, and less-sophisticated products, in relation to the firms of industrialized countries.

Tatung has served as such a conduit in the technology-transfer process. In its early stages, the company was the recipient of quite advanced technology in household appliances and consumer electronics from the United States and Japan through technical assistance with limited capital participation by a few key firms in those countries. Recently, it has assumed the role of transmitting this technology through both direct investment and technical-cooperation agreements with manufacturers in Southeast Asia. Tatung's greater cost economies and better knowledge of consumption technology in LDCs have given it an advantage over the multinationals of advanced countries in the transfer of such technology.

7.6 Summary

About ten years after the surge of DFI into Taiwan, native companies grew large enough to become MNCs themselves. On the basis of official data, the downward bias of which is well known, the United States and the ASEAN countries presently account for most of Taiwan's outward investment. In general, Taiwan's MNCs are motivated by the desire to: (1) secure material supplies; (2) supply local markets; (3) promote exports despite increasing international protectionism; and (4) gain or maintain access to the technology market.

A survey of even the limited data available indicates unmistakably that Taiwan's MNCs tend not only to be large in their own specific industries, but also to belong to some of Taiwan's largest conglomerates. While Taiwan's outward investment in the United States has been motivated primarily by the four reasons listed above, its DFI in ASEAN countries has been the result of "market factors" and the export of "appropriate technology." Among the ample evidence for this argument is our case study of Tatung, which followed very much the standard pattern by which Taiwanese native firms have become MNCs.

8

Conclusions

8.1 Summary

DFI has played an important role in Taiwan's modern economic development. This study began by exploring DFI inflow into Taiwan, its determinants, and changes in its structure. The primary focus of this study, technology transfer, has been discussed by examining the kinds of technology and the efficiency of resource allocation in terms of exports and employment. A company case history was used to illuminate the technology-transfer process; linkage effects and Taiwan's outward investment have been considered in great detail. The major findings of each aspect of this study are as follows.

First, DFI in Taiwan has increased since 1960, with one-fourth of that investment coming from overseas Chinese and the balance from the United States (31 percent), Japan (24 percent), and Europe (13 percent) as of 1987. Of these different foreign investors, U.S. and European firms have tended to be larger in size and to have majority-owned capital structures; Japanese investors have preferred joint ventures, especially those nearly equally owned with the natives.

Pre-1965 DFI brought in 50 percent of its capital in the form of machinery, much of it very likely secondhand. Since 1965, as DFI has become more export-oriented and better established, a growing proportion of capital has taken the form of foreign exchange and retained earnings. The latter source of DFI has made local economic conditions relevant to future DFI.

As regards industrial structure, non-Chinese investors have concentrated in the manufacturing sector, particularly in the electrical and electronics industry. The investments of overseas Chinese have clustered in mature industries and in the service sector.

Second, empirical study of foreign firms' behavior in Taiwan has confirmed that foreign capital participation serves as an efficient conduit for technology transfer. As to the specific technologies imported into Taiwan through DFI, foreign firms have introduced new products and technologies in the auto and auto-parts, electrical and electronics, and plastic and plastic-products industries; they have been less active in the machinery and textile industries.

We find also that foreign investors are very likely to market their subsidiaries' exports through their worldwide networks, either exclusively or in part. Foreign subsidiaries can be established on a larger scale from the outset when they are not dependent on such exclusive export marketing systems. Finally, DFI has managed to win various concessions when applying for technical cooperation; one of the most crucial areas has been contract terms. The empirical results show that majority-owned foreign firms in the electrical and electronics industries have tended to sign longer-term and more expensive contracts for their parent companies' technologies than have national or even minority-owned firms.

Third, with respect to the neoclassical factor-proportion argument concerning foreign technology, foreign firms as a whole used more labor-intensive technology than did national ones, not because foreign firms used more capital per unit of labor in individual industries, but because they were more heavily concentrated than national firms in labor-intensive industries. Within much more narrowly defined industries, however, foreign firms' various capital-labor ratios were not significantly different from those of their national counterparts. Nevertheless, the export sectors of foreign firms, both at the industrial and at the more aggregated levels, clearly used less capital per unit of labor than their domestic sales sectors did. In line with this, foreign firms' exports created more employment per dollar of export than did their production for domestic sales.

Fourth, the Singer Company's investment in Taiwan to produce sewing machines is an instance of the successful transfer and diffusion of foreign technology in a developing country by a multinational enterprise. The establishment of Taiwan Singer in 1963 created significant potentials for backward linkage; by providing technical assistance to its suppliers, the new enterprise realized these potentials in a relatively short time. Taiwan Singer's intensive and wide-ranging technical assistance advanced the technological standard of Taiwan's entire sewing machine industry, and thereby contributed to its growth.

Several factors contributed to Taiwan Singer's success. First, the absolute technological superiority and unparalleled marketing skills of the parent company made Taiwan Singer unafraid to offer technical assistance to the national firms. Second, Taiwan's sewing-machine assemblers and parts producers were receptive to new ideas and willing to change. Finally, the technology provided by Singer involved little or no capital expenditure, and hence its diffusion was not only easier but cheaper.

There are, however, disadvantages to excessive reliance on foreign firms for continuing technical advances and the introduction of new products. Within the multinational setting, foreign firms may not enjoy the freedom necessary to make decisions about new products and processes. The national interests of host countries may also come into conflict with the global strategies of parent organizations. Thus it is essential to the continuous growth of these industries that indigenous firms develop in concert with foreign companies and that an open-door policy on DFI be maintained.

Fifth, linkages are important potential effects of DFI on host economies. Because these potentialities are not necessarily realized, however, we must separate the potential (*ex ante*) from the actual (*ex post*) effects. Empirical data for Taiwan in the 1970s show that DFI may tend to concentrate in industries with strong backward linkages. More significantly, DFI located in EPZs or controlled by non-Chinese investors had a clear tendency to import more and, hence, to form enclaves. Over time, however, the procurement policies of these firms improved greatly. Thus, while appreciable in the short run, the enclavistic side of DFI becomes insignificant in the long run, as Taiwan's experience shows.

In addition to the time factor, foreign ownership structure, export propensity, status as a producer of either final or intermediate goods, status as a "neighboring" or "distant" investor, and the scale of operation all have a bearing on foreign firms' local purchasing behavior.

Sixth, about ten years after the surge of DFI into Taiwan, native companies grew large enough to become multinational companies themselves. On the basis of official data well known for their downward bias, the United States and the ASEAN countries presently account for most of Taiwan's outward investment. In general, Taiwan's MNCs are motivated by the desire to: (1) secure supplies of materials;

(2) penetrate local markets; (3) promote exports despite increasing international protectionism; and (4) gain access to the technology market.

A survey of even the limited data available indicates unmistakably that Taiwan's MNCs tend not only to be large in their own specific industries, but also to belong to some of Taiwan's largest conglomerates. While Taiwan's outward investment in the United States has been motivated primarily by the four reasons listed above, its DFI in ASEAN countries has been the result of "market factors" and the export of "appropriate technology." Among the ample evidence for this argument is our case study of Tatung, which followed very much the standard pattern by which Taiwanese native firms have become MNCs.

8.2 Implications

In seeking to explain Taiwan's economic growth, this study has shown the importance of DFI for that growth. While Taiwan's experience is unique, being the result of the confluence of a number of different factors, its development process does exhibit features that may be relevant to other LDCs trying to build up their economies. Because other LDCs look to Taiwan as a model of successful economic development, the results of DFI in Taiwan should be investigated carefully. Many of the policies implemented by Taiwan could be applied elsewhere.

As this study shows, DFI in Taiwan has served less as an engine of growth than as a catalyst to significantly facilitate the development process. Even at the very beginning, Taiwan was never dependent upon DFI as a major source of capital; at its peak, around 1970, the DFI capital investment amounted to only 4.32 percent of the country's total, or 7.33 percent of total capital in the manufacturing sector during that time. During most of this period, DFI accounted for around 20 percent of Taiwan's total exports, and it was in the export sector that DFI played its more significant role in creating jobs. More than anything else, DFI contributed to Taiwan's economy by introducing new technology. Microeconomically, that is, with respect to improvement of the efficiency of resource allocation in both the static and the dynamic sense, DFI constantly fostered competition in the domestic market, helped to open up more foreign markets, and diffused new technologies. Thus it was not the infusion of capital that was important, but, rather, the nature of that capital and the environment that accommodated it.

Taiwan maintained an open and relatively unrestricted DFI policy. For instance, Taiwan permitted the importation of secondhand machinery as investment capital, which neither harmed the local machinery industry nor impaired the efficient use of that particular capital. Taiwan did not impose a local-content requirement on foreign firms, which, nevertheless, increased their local-purchase ratio over time. Taiwan adopted no specific DFI policy aimed at creating jobs, but it provided a reasonably good infrastructure and incentives for export-oriented DFI; this environment, in turn, helped create many job opportunities. Taiwan did not impose tight control over royalty payments, and the consequent expansion in technical cooperation created another channel for importing foreign technology. Finally, as illustrated by the Singer case, Taiwan did not grant a monopoly to the first foreign investor, however great its impact on the initial development of the industry; this policy assured the continuous inflow of foreign technology.

Several other valuable lessons are to be learned from Taiwan's experience. The less expensive an imported technology, the faster the diffusion of its technology will be. DFI in EPZs is an effective means of creating exports and jobs, but it is more dependent on imported materials than DFI by non-EPZ foreign firms. This situation should be tolerated, for it has been found that if local supply conditions permit, the reluctance to buy locally will vanish within a short time. Taiwan's growing native multinationals in LDCs, maturing by first mastering foreign technology, may import technologies more suitable than those from DCs.

Taiwan's economy is presently in a state of transition, during which the role of DFI will change. First, Taiwan's comparative advantage in the production of "conventional" goods has eroded quickly since the significant appreciation of the NT dollar and the rise in wages that began in 1986. Mainland China and other Asian LDCs are expected to supplant Taiwan in those markets. Using its widespread trade networks, Taiwan is expected to greatly accelerate its outward investment, as predicted by the product-cycle theory. In this regard, Taiwan's investment in host LDCs could be beneficial to both parties.

As a result, Taiwan's industrial structure will have to be overhauled; the pressure to develop technology- and capital-intensive industries will intensify. Taiwan is no longer short of capital but, rather, of technology; DFI will facilitate the restructuring of Taiwan's industries. It is expected that more high-tech-oriented DFI will be brought in, as it has been in the past (Schive and Hsueh 1987; Schive, forthcoming).

Another shift in DFI will take place in the service sector, particularly in the financial markets. This study has not touched on the operations of foreign banks, and the data used here do not adequately cover DFI in the banking and insurance industries. Given the highly regulated and very underdeveloped character of the financial sector of the Taiwanese economy (as judged by its small contribution to GNP), there is ample room for foreign investment in it, especially after the massive liberalization that has taken place recently.

Finally, the limitations of this study and the need for future inquiry should be pointed out. The extent to which foreign banks have influenced Taiwan's economy obviously calls for thorough investigation. At least as important are the negative externalities associated with DFI in Taiwan, for example, environmental damage and detrimental working conditions. Do foreign investors rate worse in these regards than their local counterparts? In addition, we have seen a steady withdrawal of DFI from Taiwan, around 16 percent of the arrived capital since 1970 (see table A-1). Why has this occurred? Do these failures represent anything more than investors' inability to adapt to a very fluid environment? Will this trend affect DFI in the future? A study of these instances of failure would provide more insight into the successful application of DFI.

LDCs have alternately shunned and wooed DFI, seeing it as either an infringement on national sovereignty or a way to acquire foreign technology, expertise, and capital. As this study indicates, Taiwan's experience has been very positive. While various structural changes will require some adjustments to DFI over the next few years, the same basic principles of DFI policy that have served it so well in the past will be retained. DFI will continue to act as a catalyst in future technology transfer, and thus will continue to contribute to Taiwan's economic growth.

Appendix

TABLE A-1   APPROVED AND ARRIVED DFI, 1953–1986

Year	Approved (US$ million)	Arrived (US$ million)	Repatriation of foreign capital	Investment abroad
1952	1.07	0.62		
1953	3.70	2.11		
1954	2.22	9.91		
1955	4.60	0.51		
1956	3.49	0.66		
1957	1.62	2.40		
1958	2.52	11.71		
1959	0.97	3.78		
1960	15.47	5.77		
1961	14.30	9.46		
1962	5.20	8.98		
1963	18.05	15.23		
1964	19.90	15.57		
1965	41.61	10.51		0.47
1966	29.28	9.59		1.16
1967	57.01	27.87		1.29
1968	89.89	27.89		0.60
1969	109.44	51.52		—
1970	138.90	61.93		0.53

1971	162.96	52.63		1.21
1972	126.66	36.37	9.28	3.40
1973	248.85	67.79	6.21	0.85
1974	189.38	104.05	21.89	0.86
1975	118.18	70.57	36.36	0.37
1976	141.52	90.71	20.19	3.89
1977	163.91	76.50	24.19	6.59
1978	212.93	129.74	15.88	4.16
1979	328.84	120.86	18.88	2.73
1980	465.96	190.83	29.52	45.36
1981	395.76	156.5	21.01	58.08
1982	380.01	149.18	50.43	21.84
1983	404.47	175.4	39.33	16.49
1984	558.74	231.59	80.99	70.32
1985	702.46	343.68	55.73	82.65
1986	705.57	350.22	69.22	68.50
1952–1960	35.65	41.47	—	—
1961–1970	523.58	241.59	—	4.05
1971–1980	2,159.17	940.05	182.40	69.42
1981–1986	3,147.00	1,406.57	—	317.88

SOURCES: Investment Commission, MOEA, *Statistics of Approved Overseas Chinese and Foreign Investment, Republic of China,* various issues; Central Bank of China, *Balance of Payments,* various issues.

NOTE: Pre-1958 arrived DFI included imports with self-provided foreign exchange by overseas Chinese investors.

TABLE A-2   DIRECT AND INDIRECT EXPORTS OF FOREIGN FIRMS, 1976–1985
(UNITS: $ MILLION, PERCENT)

Year	Direct exports			Indirect exports		
	Non-overseas Chinese	Total	As percent of total sales	Non-overseas Chinese	Total	As percent of total sales
1976	1,410	1,743	45.85	411	591	15.56
1977	1,534	1,961	44.05	500	748	16.80
1978	2,283	2,796	44.36	677	985	15.62
1979	2,760	3,284	39.14	881	1,272	15.16
1980	3,062	3,648	37.21	1,135	1,558	15.95
1981	3,280	4,062	39.21	1,292	1,558	15.03
1982	3,546	4,286	43.59	975	1,145	11.65
1983	2,808	3,524	39.24	796	1,017	11.32
1984	4,815	5,602	41.85	1,143	1,423	10.63
1985	3,289	3,943	39.78	728	919	9.27

SOURCE: Investment Commission, MOEA, *An Analysis of the Operations and Economic Effects of Foreign Enterprises in Taiwan*, various issues.
NOTE: Indirect exports refer to sales to downstream producers for export. These data were accurately recorded under the tariff rebate system. That system was gradually abolished in the 1980s, which may account for the declining share of indirect exports in total sales.

TABLE A-3 APPROVED OVERSEAS CHINESE AND NON-CHINESE INVESTMENT BY PERIOD, INDUSTRY, AND SOURCE (UNIT: US$1,000)

	1953–1960							
	Hong Kong		Japan		Other		Total	
	Amount	Percent	Amount	Percent	Amount	Percent	Amount	Percent
Primary sector	110	2.53	397	11.48	250	11.19	757	7.54
Agriculture and forestry			350	10.12	144	6.45	494	4.92
Fisheries and animal husbandry	110	2.53	47	1.36	106	4.74	263	2.62
Mining								
Manufacturing sector	3,969	91.26	2,385	68.93	1,703	76.27	8,057	80.23
Food and beverage processing			100	2.89	532	23.82	632	6.29
Textiles	871	20.03	1,116	32.25	188	8.42	2,175	21.64
Garments and footwear	121	2.78					121	1.20
Lumber and bamboo products	409	9.40					409	4.07
Pulp paper and products	618	14.21			369	16.52	987	9.83
Leather and fur products	22	0.51			60	2.69	82	0.82
Plastic and rubber products	100	2.30					100	1.00
Chemicals	423	9.73	260	7.50	168	7.52	851	8.47
Nonmetallic minerals	1,388	31.92	909	26.27	311	13.93	2,608	25.97
Basic metals and metal products								
Machinery, equipment, and instruments	17	0.39			75	3.36	92	0.92
Electronic and electrical appliances								

TABLE A-3   APPROVED OVERSEAS CHINESE AND NON-CHINESE INVESTMENT BY PERIOD, INDUSTRY, AND SOURCE
(UNIT: US$1,000) (continued)

	1953–1960							
	Hong Kong		Japan		Other		Total	
	Amount	Percent	Amount	Percent	Amount	Percent	Amount	Percent
Tertiary sector	270	6.21	678	19.59	280	12.54	1,228	12.23
Construction								
Trade	58	1.33					58	0.58
Banking and insurance								
Transportation			172	4.97			172	1.71
Services			299	8.64	176	7.88	475	4.73
Other	212	4.87	207	5.99	104	4.66	523	5.21
Total	4,349	100.00	3,460	100.00	2,233	100.00	10,042	100.00

SOURCES: Data before 1970 were compiled from primary data from the Investment Commission; Investment Commission, MOEA, *Statistics on Overseas Chinese and Foreign Investment,* various issues; Ming-cheng Liu, "Economic Development and Domestic Foreign Investment in Taiwan," *Bank of Taiwan Quarterly* 22, no. 4 (December 1971), pp. 40–71.

1961–1970

	Hong Kong		Japan		Other		Total	
	Amount	Percent	Amount	Percent	Amount	Percent	Amount	Percent
Primary sector	773	1.33	1,482	13.85	1,922	2.29	4,177	2.73
Agriculture and forestry	273	0.47	577	5.39	230	0.27	1,080	0.71
Fisheries and animal husbandry	500	0.86	905	8.46	1,382	1.65	2,787	1.82
Mining					310	0.37	310	0.20
Manufacturing sector	37,611	64.37	5,836	54.52	21,762	25.95	65,209	42.63
Food and beverage processing	3,255	5.57	1,907	17.82	8,695	10.37	13,857	9.06
Textiles	6,101	10.44	1,166	10.89	3,917	4.67	11,184	7.31
Garments and footwear	7,944	13.60	522	4.88	1,556	1.86	10,022	6.55
Lumber and bamboo products	1,384	2.37	115	1.07	543	0.65	2,042	1.33
Pulp paper and products	1,362	2.33	27	0.25			1,398	0.91
Leather and fur products	1,023	1.75			55	0.07	1,078	0.70
Plastic and rubber products	3,615	6.19	141	1.32	1,348	1.61	5,104	3.34
Chemicals	1,797	3.08	319	2.98	1,465	1.75	3,581	2.34
Nonmetallic minerals	2,076	3.55	921	8.60	2,187	2.61	5,184	3.39
Basic metals and metal products	2,304	3.94	369	3.45	1,101	1.31	3,774	2.47
Machinery, equipment, and instruments	2,333	3.99	25	0.23	713	0.85	3,071	2.01
Electronic and electrical appliances	4,417	7.56	324	3.03	182	0.22	4,923	3.22

TABLE A-3 APPROVED OVERSEAS CHINESE AND NON-CHINESE INVESTMENT BY PERIOD, INDUSTRY, AND SOURCE
(UNIT: US$1,000) (continued)

| | 1961–1970 | | | | | | | |
| | Hong Kong | | Japan | | Other | | Total | |
	Amount	Percent	Amount	Percent	Amount	Percent	Amount	Percent
Tertiary sector	20,037	34.30	3,386	31.63	60,165	71.76	83,588	54.64
Construction	5,235	8.96	300	2.80	8,913	10.63	14,448	9.44
Trade	452	0.77			1,390	1.66	1,842	1.20
Banking and insurance	596	1.02			8,813	10.51	9,409	6.15
Transportation	5,410	9.26	1,312	12.26	933	1.11	7,655	5.00
Services	2,232	3.82	1,590	14.85	36,094	43.05	39,916	26.09
Other	6,112	10.47	184	1.72	4,022	4.80	10,318	6.76
Total	58,421	100.00	10,704	100.00	83,849	100.00	152,974	100.00

SOURCES: Data before 1970 were compiled from primary data from the Investment Commission; Investment Commission, MOEA, *Statistics on Overseas Chinese and Foreign Investment*, various issues; Ming-cheng Liu, "Economic Development and Domestic Foreign Investment in Taiwan," *Bank of Taiwan Quarterly* 22, no. 4 (December 1971), pp. 40–71.

1971–1980

	Hong Kong		Japan		Other		Total	
	Amount	Percent	Amount	Percent	Amount	Percent	Amount	Percent
Primary sector	2,414	1.26	500	1.53	5,105	0.89	8,019	1.00
Agriculture and forestry	80	0.04			1,308	0.23	1,388	0.17
Fisheries and animal husbandry	2,285	1.20	500	1.53	9,797	0.66	6,582	0.82
Mining	49	0.02					49	0.01
Manufacturing sector	98,818	51.74	12,234	37.37	347,962	60.21	459,014	57.26
Food and beverage processing	663	0.35	629	1.92	21,132	3.66	22,424	2.80
Textiles	17,300	9.06	1,614	4.93	25,712	4.45	44,626	5.57
Garments and footwear	9,314	4.88	1,074	3.28	1,280	0.22	11,668	1.46
Lumber and bamboo products	2,069	1.08	35	0.11	13,012	2.25	15,116	1.89
Pulp paper and products	7,095	3.71			1,978	0.34	9,073	1.13
Leather and fur products	5,867	3.07			395	0.07	6,262	0.78
Plastic and rubber products	13,940	7.30	1,614	4.93	1,368	0.24	16,922	2.11
Chemicals	16,477	8.63	167	0.51	5,730	0.99	22,374	2.79
Nonmetallic minerals	5,219	2.73	2,742	8.38	266,299	46.08	274,260	34.21
Basic metals and metal products	6,859	3.59	992	3.03	3,855	0.67	11,706	1.46
Machinery, equipment, and instruments	6,386	3.34	346	1.06	2,262	0.39	8,994	1.12
Electronic and electrical appliances	7,629	3.99	3,021	9.23	4,939	0.85	15,589	1.94

(continued)

TABLE A-3   APPROVED OVERSEAS CHINESE AND NON-CHINESE INVESTMENT BY PERIOD, INDUSTRY, AND SOURCE
(UNIT: US$1,000) (continued)

	1971–1980							
	Hong Kong		Japan		Other		Total	
	Amount	Percent	Amount	Percent	Amount	Percent	Amount	Percent
Tertiary sector	89,769	47.00	20,002	61.10	224,867	38.90	334,638	41.74
Construction	47,195	24.71	9,175	28.03	20,504	3.55	76,874	9.59
Trade	2,394	1.25	100	0.31	1,189	0.21	3,683	0.46
Banking and insurance	5,060	2.65	49	0.15	37,136	6.43	42,245	5.27
Transportation	20,058	10.50	5,932	18.12	5,231	0.91	31,221	3.89
Services	7,426	3.89	4,309	13.16	159,158	27.54	170,893	21.32
Other	7,636	4.00	437	1.32	1,649	0.29	9,722	1.21
Total	191,001	100.00	32,736	100.00	577,934	100.00	801,671	100.00

1981–1988

	Hong Kong		Japan		Other		Total	
	Amount	Percent	Amount	Percent	Amount	Percent	Amount	Percent
Primary sector	368	0.16			23,446	7.60	23,814	4.02
Agriculture and forestry					1,448	0.47	1,448	0.24
Fisheries and animal husbandry	368	0.16			12,490	4.05	12,858	2.17
Mining					9,508	3.08	9,508	1.61
Manufacturing sector	73,594	32.02	11,869	22.27	164,268	53.23	249,731	42.21
Food and beverage processing	2,125	0.92	3,107	5.83	16,146	5.23	21,378	3.61
Textiles	8,062	3.51	3,795	7.12	26,746	8.67	38,603	6.52
Garments and footwear	4,545	1.98			1,947	0.63	6,492	1.10
Lumber and bamboo products	909	0.40	476	0.89	4,029	1.31	5,414	0.91
Pulp paper and products	11,442	4.98			6,543	2.12	17,985	3.04
Leather and fur products	692	0.30			1,160	0.38	1,852	0.31
Plastic and rubber products	4,567	1.99	93	0.17	14,019	4.54	18,679	3.16
Chemicals	23,443	10.20	15	0.03	14,588	4.73	38,046	6.43
Nonmetallic minerals	1,101	0.48			6,074	1.97	7,175	1.21
Basic metals and metal products	1,637	0.71	545	1.02	26,870	8.71	29,052	4.91
Machinery, equipment, and instruments	873	0.38	1,423	2.67	19,273	6.25	21,569	3.65
Electronic and electrical appliances	14,198	6.18	2,415	4.53	26,873	8.71	43,486	7.35

TABLE A-3   APPROVED OVERSEAS CHINESE AND NON-CHINESE INVESTMENT BY PERIOD, INDUSTRY, AND SOURCE
(UNIT: US$1,000) (continued)

1981–1988

	Hong Kong		Japan		Other		Total	
	Amount	Percent	Amount	Percent	Amount	Percent	Amount	Percent
Tertiary sector	155,898	67.82	41,398	77.72	120,865	39.17	318,161	53.77
Construction	3,176	1.38					3,176	0.54
Trade	25,562	11.12	378	0.71	13,071	4.24	39,011	6.59
Banking and insurance	7,168	3.12	8	0.02	55,669	18.04	62,845	10.62
Transportation	28,278	12.30			5,696	1.85	33,974	5.74
Services	84,867	36.92	39,921	74.95	39,777	12.89	164,565	27.81
Other	6,847	2.98	1,091	2.05	6,652	2.16	14,590	2.47
Total	229,860	100.00	53,267	100.00	308,579	100.00	591,706	100.00

TABLE A-4   APPROVED NON-CHINESE INVESTMENT BY PERIOD, INDUSTRY, AND SOURCE
(UNIT: US$1,000)

	1953–1960							
	USA		Japan		Other		Total	
	Amount	Percent	Amount	Percent	Amount	Percent	Amount	Percent
Primary sector			73	2.97			73	0.31
Agriculture and forestry								
Fisheries and animal husbandry								
Mining			73	2.97			73	0.31
Manufacturing sector	18,802	90.78	2,283	93.03	50	100.00	21,136	91.04
Food and beverage processing	473	2.28					473	2.04
Textiles	1,743	8.42	160	6.52			1,903	8.20
Garments and footwear	131	0.63					131	0.56
Lumber and bamboo products								
Pulp paper and products								
Leather and fur products								
Plastic and rubber products								
Chemicals	16,455	79.45	72	2.93			16,527	71.19
Nonmetallic minerals								
Basic metals and metal products								
Machinery, equipment, and instruments			500	20.37	50	100.00	550	2.37
Electronic and electrical appliances	1,551		1,551	63.21			1,551	6.68

TABLE A-4   Approved Non-Chinese Investment by Period, Industry, and Source
(Unit: US$1,000) (continued)

| | 1953–1960 | | | | | | | |
| | USA | | Japan | | Other | | Total | |
	Amount	Percent	Amount	Percent	Amount	Percent	Amount	Percent
Tertiary sector	1,910	9.22	98	4.00			2,008	8.65
Construction								
Trade								
Banking and insurance								
Transportation	28	0.14					28	0.12
Services	1,882	9.08					1,882	8.11
Other			98	4.00			98	0.42
Total	20,712	100.00	2,454	100.00	50	100.00	23,216	100.00

1961–1970

	USA		Japan		Other		Total	
	Amount	Percent	Amount	Percent	Amount	Percent	Amount	Percent
Primary sector	428	0.19			1,000	1.54	1,428	0.38
Agriculture and forestry								
Fisheries and animal husbandry	428	0.19			1,000	1.54	1,428	0.38
Mining								
Manufacturing sector	193,250	87.24	82,286	95.07	63,508	97.85	339,044	90.91
Food and beverage processing	3,577	1.61	1,526	1.76	990	1.53	6,093	1.63
Textiles			7,116	8.22			7,116	1.91
Garments and footwear	783	0.35	3,661	4.23	3,192	4.92	7,636	2.05
Lumber and bamboo products	160	0.07	245	0.28	200	0.31	605	0.16
Pulp paper and products	361	0.16	1,120	1.29			1,481	0.40
Leather and fur products	546	0.25	452	0.52			998	0.27
Plastic and rubber products	2,024	0.91	4,919	5.68	214	0.33	7,157	1.92
Chemicals	37,468	16.92	18,719	21.63	3,813	5.87	60,000	16.09
Nonmetallic minerals	4,501	2.03	2,973	3.43	282	0.43	7,756	2.08
Basic metals and metal products	5,757	2.60	6,961	8.04	884	1.36	13,602	3.65
Machinery, equipment, and instruments	2,900	1.31	4,618	5.35	4,434	6.84	11,952	3.20
Electronic and electrical appliances	35,173	61.03	29,976	34.04	49,499	76.26	214,648	57.55

TABLE A-4   Approved Non-Chinese Investment by Period, Industry, and Source
(Unit: US$1,000) (continued)

1961–1970

	USA		Japan		Other		Total	
	Amount	Percent	Amount	Percent	Amount	Percent	Amount	Percent
Tertiary sector	27,809	12.57	4,270	4.93	397	0.61	32,476	8.71
Construction	8,240	3.72	428	0.49	297	0.46	8,965	2.44
Trade	570	0.26					570	0.15
Banking and insurance	1,278	0.58					1,278	0.34
Transportation	5,294	2.39	325	0.38			5,619	1.51
Services	5,171	2.33	625	0.72			5,796	1.55
Other	7,256	3.29	2,892	3.34	100	0.15	10,248	2.76
Total	221,487	100.00	86,556	100.00	64,905	100.00	372,948	100.00

1971–1980

	USA		Japan		Other		Total	
	Amount	Percent	Amount	Percent	Amount	Percent	Amount	Percent
Primary sector	154	0.03	242	0.07	140	0.03	536	0.04
Agriculture and forestry								
Fisheries and animal husbandry	154	0.03	100	0.03	140	0.03	394	0.03
Mining			142	0.04			142	0.01
Manufacturing sector	474,993	88.94	347,219	94.19	418,951	92.12	1,241,163	91.43
Food and beverage processing	6,033	1.13	5,678	1.54	1,038	0.23	12,749	0.94
Textiles	346	0.06	21,724	5.89	2,493	0.55	24,563	1.81
Garments and footwear	2,906	0.54	2,259	0.61	3,144	0.69	8,309	0.61
Lumber and bamboo products	616	0.12	3,512	0.95	500	0.11	4,628	0.34
Pulp paper and products	1,559	0.29	638	0.17	1,054	0.23	3,251	0.24
Leather and fur products	377	0.07	347	0.09	1,269	0.28	1,993	0.15
Plastic and rubber products	15,822	2.96	18,686	5.07	3,077	0.68	37,585	2.71
Chemicals	111,632	20.90	27,730	7.52	67,852	14.92	207,214	15.26
Nonmetallic minerals	1,368	0.26	9,153	2.48	28,741	6.32	39,262	2.89
Basic metals and metal products	15,057	2.82	53,218	14.44	79,264	17.43	147,539	10.87
Machinery, equipment, and instruments	10,353	1.94	40,863	11.08	87,719	19.29	138,935	10.23
Electronic and electrical appliances	308,924	57.84	163,411	44.33	142,800	31.40	615,135	45.31

TABLE A-4   APPROVED NON-CHINESE INVESTMENT BY PERIOD, INDUSTRY, AND SOURCE
(UNIT: US$1,000) *(continued)*

	1971–1980							
	USA		Japan		Other		Total	
	Amount	Percent	Amount	Percent	Amount	Percent	Amount	Percent
Tertiary sector	58,939	11.03	21,185	5.74	35,729	7.85	115,853	8.53
Construction	63	0.01	926	0.25			989	0.07
Trade	1,072	0.20			643	0.14	1,715	0.13
Banking and insurance	34,061	6.38	570	0.15	13,841	3.04	48,472	3.57
Transportation	1,900	0.36			290	0.06	2,190	0.16
Services	18,437	3.45	7,823	2.13	12,314	2.71	38,574	2.84
Other	3,406	0.64	11,866	3.23	8,641	1.89	23,913	1.77
Total	534,086	100.00	368,646	100.00	454,820	100.00	1,357,552	100.00

1981–1988

	USA		Japan		Other		Total	
	Amount	Percent	Amount	Percent	Amount	Percent	Amount	Percent
Primary sector	5,503	0.34	2,407	0.14	2,563	0.14	10,473	0.20
Agriculture and forestry	469	0.03	289	0.02	466	0.03	1,224	0.02
Fisheries and animal husbandry	5,034	0.31	1,224	0.07			6,258	0.12
Mining			894	0.05	2,097	0.11	2,991	0.06
Manufacturing sector	1,357,188	83.42	1,445,081	82.22	1,138,485	62.01	3,940,754	75.48
Food and beverage processing	85,766	5.27	25,453	1.45	90,683	4.94	201,902	3.87
Textiles	491	0.03	21,279	1.21	10,778	0.59	32,539	0.62
Garments and footwear	603	0.04	2,826	0.16	12,598	0.69	16,027	0.31
Lumber and bamboo products	631	0.04	4,764	0.27	8,590	0.47	13,985	0.27
Pulp paper and products	13,164	0.81	5,309	0.30	1,218	0.07	19,691	0.38
Leather and fur products	1,524	0.09	517	0.03	5,254	0.29	7,295	0.14
Plastic and rubber products	10,185	0.63	121,175	6.89	67,620	3.68	198,980	3.81
Chemicals	373,921	22.98	128,261	7.30	338,207	18.41	840,389	16.09
Nonmetallic minerals	21,080	1.30	66,588	3.79	29,861	1.63	117,529	2.25
Basic metals and metal products	97,742	6.01	160,293	9.12	121,372	6.61	379,407	7.27
Machinery, equipment, and instruments	103,692	6.37	431,778	24.57	105,610	5.75	641,080	12.28
Electronic and electrical appliances	648,389	39.85	476,847	27.13	346,694	18.88	1,471,931	28.19

TABLE A-4　　APPROVED NON-CHINESE INVESTMENT BY PERIOD, INDUSTRY, AND SOURCE
(UNIT: US$1,000) *(continued)*

	1981–1988							
	USA		Japan		Other		Total	
	Amount	Percent	Amount	Percent	Amount	Percent	Amount	Percent
Tertiary sector	264,572	16.26	309,986	17.64	695,655	37.88	1,270,213	24.33
Construction			6,553	0.37	9,493	0.52	16,046	0.31
Trade	8,286	0.51	53,216	3.03	70,855	3.86	132,357	2.53
Banking and insurance	47,628	2.93	2,310	0.13	166,186	9.05	216,124	4.14
Transportation	228	0.01	1,135	0.06	130,618	7.11	131,981	2.53
Services	198,203	12.18	204,608	11.64	304,155	16.56	706,966	13.54
Other	10,227	0.63	42,164	2.40	14,348	0.78	66,739	1.28
Total	1,627,263	100.00	1,757,474	100.00	1,836,703	100.00	5,221,440	100.00

SOURCES: Same as for table A-3.

Notes

Chapter 1

1. This prediction is based on 1980 data indicating a 2–3 percent growth rate for Italy and a 5–7 percent rate for Taiwan. In 2000, Italy's per capita GNP will be between $6850 and $8418, and Taiwan's will be between $6691 and $9760 (Klein 1985).
2. By definition, DFI denotes "the amount [of capital] invested by residents of a country in foreign enterprise over which they have effective control" (Ragazzi 1973, p. 141).
3. The question of ownership arises from the ambiguity of "effective control" in the definition of DFI. Many criteria have been used to solve this problem. A cutoff point between 10 and 25 percent is frequently used, though some countries have applied that description to ventures with more than 1 percent foreign ownership (IMF 1977). In order to select a large sample for this analysis, we have defined DFI in the broadest possible sense. However, the figures referring to DFI will be weighted by foreign ownership whenever the data are available.

Chapter 2

1. There are two reasons for choosing 1952 as the beginning of Taiwan's modern economic development. First, Taiwan's agricultural and manufacturing production levels first exceeded their previous peaks around 1952 (Lee 1971). Second, Taiwan's first four-year plan began in 1952; thus more economic data are available from that year onward.

2. Toyota's initial investment had anticipated a plant assembling 200,000 cars per year in 1983 and a total capital of $500 million. The project was dropped because of disputes over export requirements, and a much smaller substitute investment of $11 million was approved two years later.

3. It could be argued that there must be some safeguard to prevent the abuse of this privilege. The question is how to implement those rules. A regulation covering the use of old machines existed in Taiwan: corporate earnings exempted from taxation because they were earmarked for expansion had to be spent for new machinery, unless special permission was granted. See article 2 of the Supplementary Law to the Statute for Encouragement of Investment.

4. The significant and swift decline in Taiwan's imports of used machinery also occurred in those of Japan. For example, Shinohara's study of the structure of Japanese industry showed that small firms employing 30–49 and 100–199 persons lowered the share of used machinery in their total fixed assets by about 10 percent between 1954 and 1958 (Sen 1962, p. 346).

Chapter 3

1. This chapter is condensed from Schive 1978, Schive 1979a, and Ranis and Schive 1985.

2. For example, in the textile and apparel industry, of a total of 11 foreign firms without foreign technology, only 4 belonged to non-Chinese investors.

3. The survey's main purpose was to study the rate of effective protection for more than 600 of Taiwan's commodities (Schive et al. 1979).

4. A transfer price policy is one which states that a foreign firm is not in itself a profit center; a multinational corporation's direct control of a subsidiary's exports and prices may serve to increase total profits.

Chapter 4

1. This chapter is drawn primarily from Schive 1981.

2. Countless studies of this important issue have been done. Three of them analyze Taiwan's data (Cohen 1973; Mason 1973; Riedel 1975). Because of either measurement problems or the limited data, the conclusions reached are not strong enough to support policy suggestions. For a critical survey of these three papers, see the appendix to this chapter.

3. For details and reasoning, see the appendix to this chapter.

4. For a detailed breakdown between overseas Chinese and non-Chinese DFI, see Ranis and Schive 1985, p. 107.

5. For a detailed analysis of the employment effects of ownership structure and paid-up capital in U.S. and Japanese DFI, see Ranis and Schive 1985, pp. 111–18.

Chapter 5

1. This chapter is taken from Schive 1979b. The lack of later data should have no effect on the validity of the discussions or conclusions.
2. The concept of time and motion study is used extensively by industrial enterprises to increase efficiency. Taiwan Singer introduced two then-new techniques in this area: the method of time measurement (MTM) and the critical path method (CPM).
3. Taiwan Singer hired fifteen inspectors in 1970, compared to the three inspectors hired by Singer's Japan subsidiary, which had a higher level of production.
4. Interview with Mr. S. K. Chang, general manager of Lihtzer.
5. These firms were: Taiwan Janome Sewing Machine Co., in 1970; Taibo Machine Co., half-owned by Nora Sewing Machine, Inc., in 1974; Brother; and Ishin Sewing Machine Co., a member of the Toyota group.

Chapter 6

1. This chapter is taken primarily from Schive 1978 and 1981.
2. For a discussion of the timing and other conditions necessary to develop secondary import-substitution industry—specifically, the intermediate-commodity and capital-goods industries in Taiwan and Korea—see Schive, forthcoming.
3. An ordinary input-output table is limited to intermediate input transactions. Every industry uses capital goods, but in the form of depreciation; therefore the forward linkages of the capital goods industry cannot be shown in the measurement formulated.
4. A similar study, applying domestic input-output tables, could be carried out to analyze the *ex post* linkages related to DFI, except that we would have to assume identical local contents for both foreign and national firms; but this is not the case (Riedel 1975) and would violate the foreign enclave assumption.
5. When local-content requirements were first introduced in 1959, a total of nine products were regulated: televisions, radios, refrigerators, transformers, cars, motorcycles, diesel engines, tractors, and air conditioners. For the effectiveness of these regulations in promoting local parts industries, see Schive, forthcoming.

Chapter 7

1. This chapter is condensed from three papers: Schive 1982, Ting and Schive 1981, and Schive and Hsueh 1985.
2. The latest survey of Taiwan's outward investment was conducted in 1982. Since the approval data are less reliable and lack much crucial information, this section will be based on the survey data.
3. Lecraw has pointed out that, in addition to these market considerations, some LDCs are politically unstable (Lecraw 1981, p. 43). For example, both Hong Kong and Taiwan face uncertain political futures because of the potential threat from the People's Republic of China. Thus, firms in these two countries will use DFI to offset domestic political risk. For purposes of testing, however, this factor may not be easy to separate from others.

References

Caves, R. E. 1971. "International Corporations: The Industrial Economics of Foreign Investment." *Econometrica* 149(February 1971): 1–27.

———. 1974. "Industrial Organization." In John H. Dunning, ed., *Economic Analysis and the Multinational Enterprise*. London: Allen & Unwin.

Chang, Chung-han. 1980. *Industrialization in Taiwan During the Colonial Period*. Taipei: United Economics.

Chen, E. K. Y. 1983. *Multinational Corporations, Technology, and Employment*. London: Macmillan.

Cohen, B. I. 1973. "Comparative Behaviour of Foreign and Domestic Export Firms in a Developing Economy." *Review of Economics and Statistics* 55(May 1973): 190–97.

———. 1975. *Multinational Firms and Asian Exports*. New Haven, Conn.: Yale University Press.

Davis, H. 1977. "Technology Transfer Through Commercial Transactions." *Journal of Industrial Economics* 16, no. 2(December 1977): 161–75.

de la Forre, José. 1974. "Foreign Investment and Export Dependence." *Economic Development and Cultural Change* 23(1974): 133–50.

Denison, Edward F. 1967. *Why Growth Rates Differ: Postwar Experience in Nine Western Countries*. Washington, D.C.: Brookings Institution.

Edwards, A. 1977. *Asian Industrial Expansion*. London: Financial Times.

Galenson, W., ed. 1979. *Economic Growth and Structure Change in Taiwan*. Ithaca, N.Y.: Cornell University Press.

——, ed. 1985. *Foreign Trade and Investment, Economic Development in the Newly Industrializing Asian Countries.* Madison, Wisc.: University of Wisconsin Press.

Hanson, J. S. 1975. "Transfer Pricing in the Multinational Corporation: A Critical Appraisal." *World Development* 3(1975): 857–63.

Helleiner, G. K. "Manufactured Exports from Less-Developed Countries and Multinational Firms." *Economic Journal* 83(1973): 21–47.

Hymer, S. 1976. *The International Operations of National Firms: A Study of Direct Foreign Investment.* Cambridge, Mass.: MIT Press.

International Monetary Fund. 1977. *Balance of Payments Manual.* 4th ed. Washington, D.C.: International Monetary Fund.

James, D. D. 1974. *Used Machinery and Economic Development.* East Lansing, Mich.: Michigan State University, International Business and Economic Studies.

Jocoby, N. H. 1966. *U.S. Aid to Taiwan: A Study of Foreign Aid, Self-Help and Development.* New York: Praeger.

Johnson, Harry G. 1968. *Comparative Cost and Commercial Policy for a Developing World Economy* (The Wicksell lectures). Stockholm: Ahnqvist S. Wicksell.

——. 1972. "Survey of the Issues." In Peter Drysdale, ed., *Direct Foreign Investment in Asia and the Pacific.* Toronto: University of Toronto Press.

Kindleberger, C. P. 1968. *American Business Abroad: Six Lectures on Direct Investment.* (New Haven, Conn.: Yale University Press.)

Klein, L. R. 1985. "Economic Strategies for Taiwan in the Remainder of This Century." In *Conference on Prospects for the Economy of Taiwan. The Republic of China in the 1980s.* Chung-li: National Central University.

——. 1986. "Introduction." In L. J. Lau, ed., *Models of Development.* San Francisco, Calif.: Institute for Contemporary Studies.

Koh, K. L. 1973. *Factors Influencing U.S. International Firms in Locating Export Oriented Manufacturing Facilities in Singapore, Taiwan and Hong Kong.* Ph.D. diss., Indiana University.

Kuo, S. W. Y. 1983. *Taiwan: Economy in Transition.* Boulder, Colo.: Westview Press.

Kuznetz, S. 1966. *Modern Economic Growth: Rate, Structure and Spread.* New Haven, Conn.: Yale University Press.

Lall, S. 1978. "Transnationals, Domestic Enterprises, and Industrial Structure in Host LDCs: A Survey." *Oxford Economic Papers* 30(July 1978): 217–48.

Lau, L. J., ed. 1986. *Models of Development.* San Francisco, Calif.: Institute for Contemporary Studies.

Lecraw, D. J. 1981. "Internationalization of Firms from LDCs: Evidence from the ASEAN Region." In K. Kumar and M. G. McLeod, eds., *Multinationals from Developing Countries* (Lexington, Mass.: Lexington Books), pp. 37–52.

Lee, T. H. 1971. *Intersectoral Capital Flows in Economic Development of Taiwan, 1895–1960.* Ithaca, N.Y.: Cornell University Press.

Leff, N. H. 1968. *The Brazil Capital Goods Industry.* Cambridge, Mass.: Harvard University Press.

Liu, C. H. 1968. "A Case Report on Promotion of National Industry Standard by Introduction of Foreign Investment." *Shing-Sheng Daily News,* 19 August, 1968.

Maddison, Angus. *Economic Progress and Policy in Developing Countries.* London: Allen & Unwin.

Marsden, K. 1970. "Progressive Technologies for Developing Countries." *International Labor Review* 101(May 1970): 475–502.

Mason, R. H. 1973. "Some Observations on the Choice of Technology by Multinational Firms in Developing Countries." *Review of Economics and Statistics* 55(August 1973):349–53.

Meier, G. M., ed. 1970. *Leading Issues in Economic Development Studies in International Poverty.* 2nd ed. Oxford: Oxford University Press.

Ministry of Economic Affairs (MOEA). 1970. *Monthly Bulletin of Industrial Production* (changed to *Industrial Production Statistics Monthly*).

Moxon, R. W. 1979. "The Cost, Conditions, and Adaptation of MNC Technology in Developing Countries." *Research in International Business and Finance* 1(1979):159–233.

Nelson, Richard R. 1974. "Less Developed Countries—Technology Transfer and Adoption: The Role of the Indigenous Scientific Community." *Economic Development and Cultural Change* 23(October 1974):61–77.

Pany, T. C., and Watson, J. F. 1979. "Technology Flows and Foreign Investment in the Australian Manufacturing Sector." *Australian Economic Papers* 18(June 1979):103–17.

Ragazzi, G. 1973. "Theories of the Determinants of Direct Foreign Investment." *International Monetary Fund Staff Papers* 20(July 1973):471–98.

Ranis, G. 1979. "Industrial Development." In W. Galenson, ed., *Economic Growth and Structural Change in Taiwan.* Ithaca, N.Y.: Cornell University Press.

Ranis, G., and Schive, C. 1985. "Direct Foreign Investment in Taiwan's Development." In W. Galenson, ed., *Foreign Trade and Investment.* Madison, Wisc.: University of Wisconsin Press.

Rassmussen, P.N. 1956. *Studies in Inter-Sectoral Relations.* Amsterdam: North Holland Publisher.

Rhee, Y. W., and Westphal, L. E. 1978. "A Note on Exports of Technology from the Republic of China and Korea." *World Bank.*

Riedel, J. 1975. "The Nature and Determinants of Export-Oriented DFI in a Developing Economy: A Case Study of Taiwan." *Weltwirtschaftliches Archiv* 1975:505–28.

Schive, C., Yeh, R. S., Wu, C. C., You, K. M., and Lin, K. S. 1979. *A Study of Effective Protection of Important Commodities in the Republic of China* (in Chinese). [Taipei]: Research, Development and Evaluation Commission, Executive Yuan, Republic of China.

Schive, C. 1978. *Direct Foreign Investment, Technology Transfer and Linkage Effects: A Case Study of Taiwan.* Ph.D. diss., Case Western University.

————. 1979a. "Direct Foreign Investment and Transfer of Technology: Theories and Taiwan's Evidence." In *Proceedings of the National Science Council 3,* no. 4(1979):455–8.

————. 1979b. "Technology Transfer Through Direct Foreign Investment: A Case Study of Taiwan Singer." *Proceedings of the Academy of International Business: Asia-Pacific Dimension of International Business* (Honolulu).

————. 1979c. *A Study of Economic Impact of Direct Foreign Investment in the Republic of China* (in Chinese). [Taipei]: Research, Development and Evaluation Commission, Executive Yuan, Republic of China.

————. 1981. "A Study of Foreign Firms' Local Purchasing Behavior: Its Relation to the Development of the Secondary Import Substitution Industry in Taiwan" (in Chinese). In *Proceedings, Trade and Taiwan's Economic Development* (Taipei: Academia Sinica).

————. 1982a. *A Report of Private Outward Investment* (in Chinese). [Taipei]: Investment Commission, Ministry of Economic Affairs.

————. 1982b. "Direct Foreign Investment and Host Country Technology: A Factor Proportion Approach in Taiwan." *Economic Essays* 10(June 1982):211–27.

————. 1983. "Direct Foreign Investment, Technology Transfer and Industrial Development in Taiwan" (in Chinese). In *Proceedings, Industrial Development in Taiwan* (Taipei: Academia Sinica).

————. 1986. *A Review of Economic Impact of Foreign Enterprises in Taiwan* (in Chinese). Taipei: Investment Commission, Ministry of Economic Affairs, Republic of China.

————. 1987. "Trade Patterns and Trends of Taiwan." In Colin I. Bradford and William H. Branson, eds., *Trade and Structural Changes in Pacific Asia.* Chicago, Ill.: University of Chicago Press.

————. In press. "The Next Stage of Industrialization in Taiwan and Korea." In Mary Gereffi and Don Wyman, eds., *Development Strategies in Latin America and East Asia.* Princeton, N.J.: Princeton University Press.

Schive, C., and Hsueh, K. T. 1985. "Taiwan's Investment in the ASEAN Countries" (working paper).

————. 1987. "The Experience and Prospects of High-Tech Industry Development in Taiwan, R.O.C.—The Case of the Information Industry." In *1987 Joint Conference on the Industrial Policies of the Republic of China and the Republic of Korea.* Taipei: Chung-hua Institution for Economic Research.

Schive, C., and Yeh, R. S. 1980. "Direct Foreign Investment and Taiwan's TV Industry." *Economic Essays* 9, no. 2(November 1980):261–91.

Schreiber, J. D. 1970. *U.S. Corporate Investment in Taiwan.* Cambridge, Mass.: Harvard University Press.

Schumacher, E. F. 1973. *Small Is Beautiful: A Study of Economics as if People Mattered.* London: Blond & Briggs.

Simon, D. F., and Schive, C. 1986. "Taiwan." In F. W. Rushing and C.G. Brown, eds., *National Policies for Developing High Technology Industries: International Comparison*. Boulder, Colo.: Westview Press; also in *Economic Essays-*(June 1985): 153-80.

Solow, R. 1957. "Technological Change and the Aggregate Pridurtion Function." *Review of Economics and Statistics* 39(1957):313-20.

Spencer, Daniel L. 1970. *Technology Gap in Perspective: Strategy of International Technology Transfer*. New York: Spartan Books.

Spencer, Daniel L., and Woroniak, Alexander, eds. 1967. *The Transfer of Technology to Developing Countries*. New York: Praeger.

Strassmann, W. P. 1968. *Technological Change and Economic Development: The Manufacturing Experience of Mexico and Puerto Rico*. Ithaca, N.Y.: Cornell University Press.

Svennilson, Ingvar. 1967. "The Strategy of Transfer." In Daniel L. Spencer and Alexander Woroniak, eds., *The Transfer of Technology to Developing Countries*. New York: Praeger.

Taiwan Industrial Production Statistics Monthly (published by the Ministry of Economic Affairs of the Republic of China).

Ting, W. L., and Schive, C. 1981. "Direct Investment and Technology Transfer from Taiwan." In K. Kumar and M. C. McLeod, eds., *Multinationals from Developing Countries* (Lexington, Mass.: Lexington Books), pp. 101-14.

Vernon, R. 1966. "International Investment and International Trade in the Product Cycle." *Quarterly Journal of Economics* 80(1966):190-207.

———. 1977. *Storm Over the Multinationals*. London: Macmillan.

Weiskopf, R., and Wolff, E. 1977. "Linkages and Leakages: Industrial Tracking in an Enclaved Economy." *Economic Development and Cultural Change* 25 (July 1977): 607-28.

Wells, L. T., Jr. 1978. "Foreign Investment from the Third World: The Experience of Chinese Firms from Hong Kong." *Columbia Journal of World Business* (Spring 1978).

———. 1983. *Third World Multinationals*. Cambridge, Mass.: MIT Press.

Wickard, O. E., and Freidlin, J. N. 1976. "U.S. Investment Abroad in 1975." *Survey of Current Business* (August 1976).

Wu, R. I., and associate. 1980. *The Economic Impact of U.S. Corporate Investment in Taiwan*. [Taipei]: Academia Sinica, Institute of American Studies.

Index